FRANCHISING

FRANCHISING

**Get Your Own Business
and Be Your Own Boss
for under $5000**

by Dr. Alfred Modica

New York   London

Copyright (c) Quick Fox 1981

All rights reserved.

Printed in the United States of America.

International Standard Book Number: 0-8256-3203-X
Library of Congress Catalog Card Number: 80-52716

No part of this book may be reproduced or transmitted in any form or by any means, electronic or mechanical, including photocopying, without permission in writing from the publisher: Quick Fox, 33 West 60th Street, New York 10023.

In Great Britain: Book Sales Ltd., 78 Newman Street, London W1P 3LA.
In Canada: Gage Trade Publishing, P.O. Box 5000, 164 Commander Blvd.,
        Agincourt, Ontario M1S 3C7.

Designed by Kay Susmann

Contents

How to Own Your Own Business with Limited Capital

Today, more than ever before, people have a primary need—a need for expert guidance, sound practical gut-level guidance on starting a business of their own and doing it with limited capital. This book is written for those people in all walks of life who have a compelling reason for wishing to go into their own business. Some who thought their future secure with many years on the job are suddenly fired. Others hold low-paying jobs which aren't enough to take care of their daily overhead, let alone provide them with long-range security—people living on the so-called razor's edge where even small adversities can cause them and their families severe economic distress.

All these people have one thing in common: They seek a business opportunity that can be profitable, one that they can control themselves rather than having to rely on others to provide for their security and mold their future. There are literally millions of individuals today

who feel insecure, who are frightened about their present job or their long-term prospects. All seek expert advice, and they need it right now.

Some of you may have been burned by the wrong so-called business opportunity. You certainly cannot gamble with the small amount of capital you have accumulated—hard-earned savings eroded by today's high inflation rate, when every dollar earned during preinflation days is now worth fifty cents, based on the preinflation standard of living.

The questions most people ask of me are

1. What kind of business should I look for?

2. Where will I find the opportunity?

3. Will I be able to afford it with minimum capital?

4. How do I judge my personal suitability for the business?

5. Should I buy a going business or start one of my own?

6. Do I want a part-time or full-time business?

These are important questions, and the purpose of this book is to provide the sincere practical answers that they demand.

One basic query I always get is: Should I buy a franchise operation? Would it be more feasible than going it alone? Depending on your particular circumstance, the answer to both could be yes. It would, however, be a qualified yes—qualified by the following considerations:

1. Are you willing and able to pay the substantial goodwill fees involved in the purchase of an existing business?

2. Do you have the time and necessary expertise to fully research the enterprise and find the possible danger signs, the important hidden problems that could wipe out your investment overnight?

Now the same situation applies to many franchises that often require high fees just to enter the business—the franchisor being a substantial partner thereafter, getting a big chunk of the franchisee's earnings for the remainder of the life of the business.

You will learn in the course of reading this book that many so-called franchises can be duplicated so as to avoid those large fees. Many of you have precious little money and time with which to speculate and do not have the expertise or the patience to examine the accounting figures, marketing plans, and legal documents of an existing business or franchise. This book will help you decide whether or not it is a viable business opportunity, where to find the answers, how to make an intelligent decision, and if you are emotionally and physically attuned to owning your own business. Buying an existing or franchise business can present these serious problems:

1. The starting cost.

2. The background of the business—the worms in the woodwork that are discovered later.

3. The potential of the business—possibly it is an outmoded business that has fallen victim to a new or better idea, different competition, or a changing demand.

4. Furthermore, because of the substantial investment required, you may be entering the business with "running scared" money, and that puts two strikes against you right from go.

Two objectives—among others—of this book is to try to help you pick the business suited to you and to give hints on how to establish your business. If financing is needed, the book will point out possible sources where capital can be obtained—such as how to leverage your capital by the OPM method (other people's money).

If you get into your car and drive a few miles down a highway and then along Main Street in any fair-sized town, you will pass an array of different business establishments. On the highway, you'll probably pass an automobile dealership, gasoline stations, restaurants, maybe even a motel. In town, you'll see a hardware store, a drug store, a dry cleaner, and a real estate office, among others. You'll also pass a small office building, which provides space for other businesses.

All of these businesses have been there for some time. You know they have, for your home town has them too and at one time or another you've patronized many of them. You might even be on a first-name basis with some of the proprietors.

What you may not know is that many of these businesses are franchises—franchises in which each proprietor has certain rights spelled out in a contract with a franchisor. Each contract is different because each one covers a different kind of business. The contracts may even differ among proprietors in the same type of business, because no two franchisors operate in the same way.

Going into business for yourself requires caution—be it in a franchise or not—but just like some of those people in your own home town, there are hundreds of thousands of others throughout the United States who have gone into business for themselves as franchisees.

If you want to be your own boss, don't overlook franchising. The opportunity is there.

The automobile industry was one of the first to go into franchising, with General Motors opening franchises as early as 1898.

How to Own Your Own Business with Limited Capital

4

Isaac Merritt Singer, founder of the Singer company. Pictured is an early Singer sewing machine marketed through independent owner-operator outlets.

The History of Franchising

Franchising is often regarded as one of the "newer" marketing concepts on the American business scene. Actually the franchise concept is not new at all. Traditional franchising began in this country in 1863, when the Singer Company began using independent owner-operators to distribute its line of sewing machines.[1] General Motors began marketing its automobiles through the franchise system in 1898 and Rexall was franchising drug stores in 1901.[2] These were followed by other large companies in the petroleum, soft-drink bottling, auto accessory, and variety store fields.

The soft-drink franchise system had its beginning in the 1890s. The shipping of soft drinks in bottles was expensive, and the producers needed a more economical way to get their product to market. The answer lay in shipping syrup to franchisees who, following strict quality control procedures, produced and bottled the final product and then sold it to retailers.

During the 1930s, the large petroleum companies found that they lacked the flexibility to adjust quickly enough to rapidly changing local market conditions. (The period was characterized by price wars among gasoline outlets, and the independent dealers were not restricted to a

policy which originated in some far-off corporate headquarters.) Sales volume improved when a franchise system was established in which the operators were granted more decision-making authority.

The depression-ridden years of the thirties also saw the development of franchise systems in the drug store business and in automotive parts, food, variety goods, and hardware. Walgreens, Western Auto, Super Valu, and Ace Hardware are some of the franchisors whose names became prominent in those years.

The period following World War II—particularly the 1950s—was one of continued expansion in franchising. New roads were built, the suburbs experienced great population growth, and—in those affluent years immediately following the end of the war—families became more mobile than ever and took to the road. Highway shopping centers were developed, and families began to look away from home for outlets with familiar names whose standards of quality, price, and service were known.

What is truly new about franchising is the phenomenal growth of franchised businesses in all areas of marketing. To get an idea of the speed of the growth of franchise companies, consider this statistic: 90 percent of all franchise companies now in operation began in business

Walgreens drug stores became nationally known in the 1930s by selling through the franchise system. This is the first Walgreens, opened in Chicago in 1901.

after 1954.[3] The 1950s marked the beginning of many of the franchise giants that have become "household words" in the American economy. Specifically, the major franchises which began in the 1950s were Dunkin Donuts (1950), Holiday Inns (1952), McDonald's (1955), Kentucky Fried Chicken (1955), and Aamco Transmission Centers (1958).[4] There was a reason why the franchise boom began and thrived when it did. After World War II, many small center-city merchants became aware that their very existence was being threatened by new competitive stores in highway shopping centers. To compete, these small merchants began looking for a way to protect themselves. This created a pool of new entrepreneurs, eager to try new methods to improve their economic standing. To their ranks were added newcomers to business — returning veterans, displaced farmers, and the like. These individuals were the new franchisees who would make the franchise system viable.[5]

The growth of franchising continued in the 1960s and 1970s, and entire business systems flourished. Between 1969 and 1978 the number of franchising companies — excluding the automobile, gasoline, and soft drink businesses — increased from 600 to 1,100, the number of franchisee-owned establishments from 315,000 to 380,000, and sales from $95 billion to $239 billion.[6]

The growth was most pronounced in retailing, particularly in the fast-food business. While many major department stores were busy opening branches in the suburbs, the fast-food companies had invaded the cities. By expanding both luncheon and breakfast menus, the movement met with great success.

These years were not without their problems, however. Unethical franchisors appeared on the scene who seemed more interested in selling franchises than in offering quality goods and services, and the training and marketing support needed by inexperienced newcomers. State legislatures began looking at franchising, and by 1979 fourteen states had enacted laws to protect the franchisee. The Federal Trade Commission issued regulations — effective in October 1979 — which prohibited certain practices by franchisors and set standards for information disclosure to potential franchisees.

Another recent development has been the growth of both franchisor and franchisee associations. These associations give members a forum in which to discuss common problems. Over 370 franchisors in various businesses belong to the International Franchise Association. Franchisee associations tend to be organized by members within a single company's system. They can be extremely helpful, particularly for new franchisees.

The Concept of Franchising

You say you want to go into business for yourself? Be your own boss? Make a lot of money? You're not alone — that idea has an almost magic appeal to countless numbers of other people, too, and it always had. Every year thousands of ambitious people start businesses of their own. Some succeed; many others fail.

Like all those other ambitious people, you're willing to work hard and invest your money. But you're a practical person and — before investing your time and money — you'd like the odds in your favor. That's why you bought this book.

You've been in some of these fast-food restaurants which seem to be everywhere today and you understand that many of these restaurants

How to Own Your Own Business with Limited Capital

are really franchises, each run by an independent businessman. Most of these businesses seem to be booming.

Just what is a franchise? Can you make a good income by getting involved in something called a franchise? Yes, you can. In 1979, the average pretax income for the owner of one of the better-known fast-food restaurants was $70,000 a year, and that was in the first year of operation.[7] Many of the owners of these franchises are millionaires today. They—like you—started with limited capital, so the opportunity is there. The secret is simple—find a discipline system built on mutual trust.

You might think that "franchise" is a relatively new word used only to define a special kind of business. On the contrary, the word has been with us a long, long time. The *Oxford English Dictionary* traces it as far back into history as the thirteenth century. Franchise denoted individual freedom and liberty, immunity or exemption from a legal burden or from the jurisdiction of a particular tribunal. A franchise was a *privilege* or a *right* granted by a sovereign power to a person or body of persons. Citizenship became a franchise, as did the right to vote. Particularly in the United States, its meaning has come to include the rights conferred upon a company for some purpose of public utility. When you hear that a cable television company has been granted a franchise, it has been given the rights by a local government to operate in a specific geographic area over which that governmental body has jurisdiction. Or when a group of people representing a professional sports team from a particular city is granted a franchise in a league, they are granted the rights of membership, subject to the conditions imposed upon them by the league.

As can be seen from its usage over the years, "franchise" implies a *legal* right. A citizen of the United States has certain legal rights as defined in the constitution and statutory law. But with those rights, the citizen has certain obligations: namely, to obey the law. If the law is violated, a penalty must be paid. An understanding or an agreement exists between government and its citizens.

A franchise, as a business arrangement, also entails legal rights as defined in a contract. A contract is also an agreement, but not all agreements are contracts. To acquire the legal status of a contract, the agreement must be between competent parties. The primary requisite of competency is legal age, which in most states of the United States is eighteen years. The agreement must be for a lawful purpose, and there must be an offer and the acceptance of that offer between the parties involved. Finally, there must be a consideration—something of value, such as money or services to be rendered. A contract may be oral or written, but to avoid misunderstanding and to provide for the protection of the parties to the contract, it is preferable that it be in writing.

If you become involved in a franchise, an early step will be your signature on a contract.

Franchising is not a business or an industry—it is a method of doing business. Franchising is a *system of distribution* in which a supplier grants to another party the *right* or *privilege* to market its product or service under mutually agreed-upon conditions, over a certain period of time, and in a specified location or area. The supplier is the *franchisor;* the receiver of the right, the *franchisee;* and the right or privilege, the *franchise.* "The network, or chain, of retail units individually owned by franchisees and headed by a parent firm, or franchisor, is called a *franchise system.*"[8]

Basic Franchise Categories

Franchising is widespread, and you will probably be surprised to learn that many of the businesses from which you have purchased goods and service are—in some form or another—parts of a franchise system. Franchise systems can be classified in four basic categories:[9]

Type I. The Manufacturer-Retailer System.

Manufacturers in this system primarily include the automobile manufacturers and producers of petroleum products. The franchisees are the automobile dealerships and the gasoline outlets.

Type II. The Manufacturer-Wholesaler System.

This system is distinguished by the fact that franchisees do not sell to the consumer, but to retailers. This is the soft-drink system in which bottlers wholesale to the retail trade.

Type III. The Wholesaler-Retailer System.

Franchisors in this system are not only manufacturers, but also purchasers of other products which are distributed through licensed retail outlets. The tire manufacturers are typical of this system. Retailers may sell not only tires, batteries, and accessories, but also items such as gardening equipment. This system also includes hardware chains, drug chains, and many others.

Type IV. The Trademark/Trade Name Licensor.

This is the system typified by the comprehensive or entire business format franchise described earlier. Franchisors are not manufacturers and are usually not wholesalers. They distribute a product or group of products or services—or some combination of the two under one trade name.

This system includes restaurant chains, motel chains, and franchisees offering a host of services such as business aids, dry cleaning, and automobile rental, to name only a few.

Avis car rentals is one of the largest franchisors using the type IV category of franchising.

How to Own Your Own Business with Limited Capital

The rights of franchisees can vary widely. One factor is the type of product or service being distributed by the franchisor. An automobile manufacturer grants a *product franchise* to a franchisee (dealer) to sell its cars. The dealer operates under a company name of his or her own choosing and is generally permitted considerable discretion in running the business. It is usually an exclusive franchise; that is, no one else is given the right to sell the same line of cars in a specified location. However, because the franchise is exclusive, the dealer may have to agree to sell no other line of cars.

A product franchise can also be termed *selective*. A selective franchise is one in which the franchisee is licensed (given the right) to sell a manufacturer's products with no restrictions as to other lines that may also be sold. Jewelry, cosmetics, and electrical appliances are the products typically marketed this way. Again, the franchisees operate under their own company name and are allowed complete freedom in the running of the business.

Generally, franchisors are owners of products or services identified by brand names or trademarks. Most people are familiar with names such as *McDonald's*, *Burger King*, or *Avis* and *Hertz*. In fact, the trademark or trade name has been called "the cornerstone of the franchise system."[10] In contracts with the owners of such well-known names, the franchisee must usually agree not only to operate under that name, but also to run the business in a prescribed manner. Training school, where the franchisee is taught management techniques according to an operations manual, may be involved. The franchisee may be required to make purchases from the supplier's warehouse or from other specifically designated sources. Quality control procedures are often mandated, and the franchisee is expected to take part in marketing and advertising programs designed by the franchisor. Franchisors like these distribute not just a product or service, but complete business systems, which have come to be known as comprehensive or entire business format franchises.

Franchise rights are also granted for specific periods of time and for a specific location or area. An entrepreneur just beginning to develop a franchise system is often quite lenient with these rights. Burger King initially granted rights for ninety-nine years. Geographic rights have been given for entire states or even larger regional areas. Subfranchising is another option: franchisees are given the right by the franchisor to sell franchises; in some cases, the franchisees have become almost as big and powerful as the franchisors.

In well-established franchise systems with many outlets, rights are rarely as extensive. Five- to ten-year licenses are not uncommon, and franchisees are generally not permitted to open other outlets without prior approval—and then such rights are subject to explicit conditions.

Franchisees must pay an initial franchise fee and agree to return usually 3 to 10 percent of gross profits to the franchisor as a royalty. In addition, the franchisee might be required to contribute a percentage of profits to cover advertising costs. If the supplier owns the building and the site on which it is located, there is usually also a rent.

Despite the imposition of such fees and the varying amounts of control exercised by the supplier, franchisor-franchisee relationships are considered to be between independent businesses. According to court rulings on such relationships, a franchisee is generally not considered an employee of the franchisor, but someone who is run-

Eskimo Radiator Mfg. Company. The auto supply industry followed the automobile industry into the early use of the product franchise method of distribution.

How to Own Your Own Business with Limited Capital

ning her or his own business, subject to the conditions agreed to in the franchise contract.

Summary and Conclusions

From its beginnings in 1863, franchising as a means of distribution has spread throughout the country. Following World War II—particularly since the 1950s—most of today's franchisors became established. The 1960s and 1970s saw a tremendous growth in the number of people who went into business for themselves as franchisees. The 1980s offer continuing franchising growth and opportunities to individuals seeking wider distribution for their products and services.

Energizing the Economy

Specialization Pays Off

Franchising has made specializing a fine—and profitable—art. Some of the success of franchising can be attributed to consumer impatience. Technological advances and the demand for more expertise in limited areas of knowledge is another reason.

Franchised automobile repair service outlets have capitalized on such demands. Today there are specialists in auto body repair, painting, and the repair of brakes, transmissions, and front ends as well as tune-up, muffler, and exhaust system specialists. Employees can be trained to perform a limited service and—by specializing—a franchisee can stock an inventory of needed parts so that the car owner can have repairs done quickly.

One of the many franchises in the rapidly growing photo copying field.

Fast-food franchise systems owe a good part of their success to their ability to provide quick service at reasonable prices. The menus are limited, *and a chef is not required.* There is a virtual production-line system involved in filling a customer's order—and almost anyone can be taught how to do it.

Business is faced with constantly rising employee costs. Not only have base salaries and wages increased, but so have social security contributions. More and more employee groups are demanding—and receiving—such benefits as life and hospitalization insurance and pension programs. An employer can reduce these costs by keeping the full-time staff to a minimum and then contracting with a temporary employee agency during peak periods. Alert to this trend in business, some of these agencies became franchisors and developed very successful franchise systems.

The number of families in which both husband and wife are working has steadily increased. Such families need someone else to perform a host of services quickly and conveniently. By recognizing such needs, franchisors have established successful systems in such areas as home care, lawn care, dry cleaning, laundering, and many others.

Businesses, too—particularly smaller ones—take advantage of franchised services in accounting, tax preparation, and bookkeeping.

Almost any service, product, or family of products, it seems, can be distributed by franchising.

Franchising's Contribution to the American Economy

By its very nature, franchising is a form of business venture which contributes to the creation of new business units. As new business units are created, they become important providers of jobs.

Franchise sales of goods and services by all franchising companies

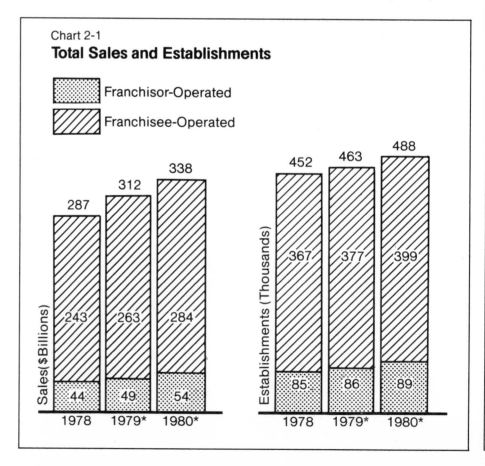

Chart 2-1
Total Sales and Establishments

are expected to reach $338 billion in 1980, an increase of 18 percent over the sales reported for 1978, while the number of establishments will be approximately 488,000 in 1980, up from 452,000 in 1978. Employment in franchising, including part-time workers and working proprietors, is estimated at 4,496,250 in 1978, a gain of over 8 percent from the 1977 level of 4,150,759 (see charts 2-1 and 2-2).[1]

Franchising has had its greatest impact in retail sales. Estimated 1979 retail sales of 279 billion dollars by franchise-associated firms accounted for almost 32 percent of all retail sales in the country. It is expected that this figure will increase by another 7 percent, to a level of 299 billion dollars, in 1980. Retail franchising accounts for 89 percent of all franchising gross receipts.

The Department of Commerce has perhaps best summarized why franchising has become such a dramatic success:
Franchising has achieved a phenomenal growth rate over the past several-years and continues to offer tremendous opportunities to individuals and companies seeking wider distribution for their products and services. Franchising has become highly attractive to many large corporations and conglomerates, here and abroad, as a means of diversification in such fields as fast food, real estate, and hotels and motels. In addition, franchisees are enjoying a competitive edge over the small business entrepreneurs by the use of trade names, marketing expertise, acquisition of a distinctive business appearance, standardization of products and services, training, and advertising support from the parent organization.

It is interesting to note that franchising has become of increasing interest to large corporations. Strong foreign competition has created a wave of mergers and acquisitions by such firms to ensure continued profitability. Franchising systems have not escaped their attention. Pillsbury has acquired Burger King; General Foods, Burger Chef;

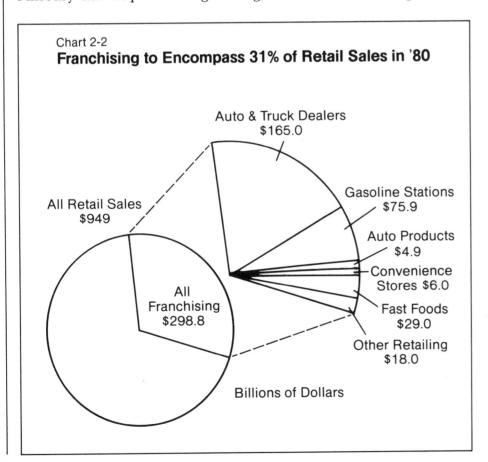

Chart 2-2
Franchising to Encompass 31% of Retail Sales in '80

Auto & Truck Dealers
$165.0

Gasoline Stations
$75.9

All Retail Sales
$949

Auto Products
$4.9

Convenience Stores $6.0

All Franchising
$298.8

Fast Foods
$29.0

Other Retailing
$18.0

Billions of Dollars

Energizing the Economy

United Fruit, Baskin & Robbins; Pepsico purchased Taco Bell and Pizza Hut; and Pet acquired Stuckey's. Manpower, the big employment agency system, is owned by Parker Pen; Weight Watchers by H. J. Heinz; and Midas by I. C. Industries. Not to be outdone, Heublein bought Kentucky Fried Chicken and Hershey's acquired Friendly's Family Restaurants. These examples represent only some of big business's movement into franchising. It is a trend that should continue into the future.

Contribution by Franchise Type

As a method of distribution, the term *franchising* embraces a wide variety of types of businesses. Depending on the type of product or service involved—or a system's stage of development—a franchise can be purchased for as little as a few hundred dollars or for as much as several million dollars.[2]

The U.S. Department of Commerce distinguishes between "traditional" franchising and "newer types" of franchising. The traditional ones are in types I and II, as described in the previous chapter—the automobile and truck dealers, gasoline service stations and soft-drink bottlers. These systems dominate the franchise field. Sales in 1977 totaled 198 billion dollars, and 1978 sales of 255 billion dollars accounted for almost 75 percent of total franchise sales in the country. The expectation for 1980 is that these categories will produce sales of an estimated 255 billion dollars, compared with 241 billion in 1979.

Seven-Eleven is a prime example of the successful retail convenience food outlet. Retailing accounts for more than 90 percent of total franchising sales.

These figures reflect the hope of a particularly strong performance by automobile and truck dealers, but the final outcome in 1980 could be decidedly different—particularly for those dealers selling American-made vehicles. Rapidly increasing prices coupled with a recession, higher unemployment, and constantly rising gasoline prices will make it difficult for the American automobile and truck industry to achieve a volume in 1980 close to the 241 billion dollars of sales achieved in 1979. These problems have caused an upsurge in the demand for more fuel-efficient cars, and the American automobile industry will not complete the retooling required to produce such cars in volume until 1981 at the earliest. Some dealerships have already closed.

There were about 210,000 type I and II franchised outlets in 1977. By 1980, this figure had already dropped to an estimated 191,390 units—due primarily to the merger of franchised bottling plants and the closing of gasoline service stations. Even with increased sales of foreign-made cars, it is quite possible that the total number of franchised units in these two categories will decline even further in 1981.

The entire business format franchise system is that which the Department of Commerce refers to as the new type of franchising. This is the type IV system—made up of trademark/trade name licensors and their franchisees. Their relationship is fully integrated—that is, it includes not only product and service under one trade name, but also a prescribed system of operation, quality control standards, and a marketing strategy and plan. This is the category that includes fast-food restaurants, nonfood retailers, lodging, personal and business services, automotive products and services, renting services, and the relatively new—and rapidly growing—real estate system.

Between 1977 and 1979, while type I and II systems experienced a decline of about 6,000 outlets, the entire business format systems grew by an estimated 47,000 units. This growth was from a base of 241,000 units in 1977 to about 288,000 outlets two years later. Estimated for 1980: 297,000 outlets.

Many of the giants of franchising belong to these newer types of systems. Their names are well known—if not nationally, at least in the regions where they are found. They include McDonald's, Aamco, Midas, H & R Block, Century 21, Taylor Rental, Ben Franklin Stores, and Holiday Inns. It is the large franchisors such as these which dominate the category. Only forty-seven franchise companies accounted for almost half the type IV sales in 1977 with their volume of 27 billion dollars. Their reported 132,000 outlets made up 55 percent of this type's total units in the same year.

The Role of Retailing

If franchising accounts for almost one-third of all retail sales in the United States, it is natural to assume that retailing represents an important segment of all franchising. An important segment it is indeed. In 1979, retailing accounted for an estimated 90 percent of total franchising sales volume.

Because retailing does play such a major role in franchising, a separate look at some of the more important retail systems is in order.

Fast Foods

Fast-food restaurants are what most people think of when they hear the word "franchise." And why not? They seem to be everywhere, and to say that Americans have taken to them with enthusiasm is an understatement. In 1979, there were just under 59,928 franchised fast-food outlets satisfying consumer demand for their wares; this is expected to rise to about 67,000 units in 1980.

As a provider of jobs, fast-food franchising not only accounted for almost 30 percent of total franchise employment in 1977, it accounted for 32 percent of all persons employed in eating and drinking establishments in the United States. Moreover, the total Franchised Restaurant employment figure of over 1,230,000 was larger than that working in any other franchise sector.

While the number of franchises in the fast-food restaurant field have increased dramatically, so has that of new franchisors. While six franchisors went out of business in 1977 and an additional six decided to abandon franchising, forty-seven new companies entered franchising for the first time. That brought the total number of franchisors of all types of restaurants to three hundred and fifty—a new industry high.

The large corporations that now own some of these franchise systems, such as General Foods, Pepsico, Pillsbury, and Heublein, are very adroit marketers. Their expertise in marketing research, advertising, and promotion has already greatly affected the systems they own and, therefore, the entire fast-food restaurant business. It's a big business and a very competitive business. Some of America's largest and most prestigious advertising agencies assist in developing advertising and promotional strategy. It has been said that marketing in a franchise system entails four P's: product, price, packaging, and promotion. The product—with help from market research—is the menu the consumer wants, at a sensible price. The package—in franchising—is the exterior architecture and the interior decor. And try turning on a television set or radio without being exposed to fast-food advertising! One function of advertising is to build brand loyalty. In the fast-food business, it's attempting to build restaurant loyalty.

While each chain tends to specialize in certain food types, menus have been expanded to satisfy customer desires and capture more breakfast and dinner business. Like any other business, restaurants have been faced with rising costs. Menu expansion is an attempt to combat these costs by increasing customer traffic and the size of the average check.

Although menus are expanding, fast-food restaurants are still classified by the food type in which they tend to specialize. In addition, fast-food restaurant successes have led to the development of franchised systems in what are referred to as family-style restaurants, dinner-style restaurants, and pancake houses. Some of these specialize, others do not. Some are full-service establishments, others offer both fast food and full service.

Chart 2-3 lists the various types of franchised restaurants and the largest—by total number of franchisees—of each. Note that seven franchisors claimed over a thousand franchised outlets in 1979, while an eighth claimed over nine hundred.

Convenience Food Stores

These are the smaller grocery and supermarket-type stores, and there were 15,200 such franchised outlets in 1978 which produced sales of 4.8 billion dollars. Like the big-chain company-owned supermarkets, these convenience food stores are trying to develop ways to combat the inroads into their business made by the fast-food restaurants. Offering take-out food—including precooked dishes requiring only a quick

Chart 2-3

19

The Largest Restaurant Franchisors
By Type and Number of Franchisees
1979

Type	Franchisor	Number of Franchisees
Hamburger specialty	McDonald's	4173
	Burger King	2000
	Wendy's	1385
	Sonic Industries	1126
	Burger Chef	559
	All-American Burger	500
Fried Chicken specialty	Kentucky Fried Chicken	3520
	Golden Skillet Companies	250
Pizza & Italian Food	Pizza Hut	1907
	Shakey's	470
Mexican specialty	Taco John's	239
	Taco Time	197
Submarine sandwiches	Blimpies	250
Miscellaneous fast foods	A & W Restaurants	1353
	Arby's International	788
	Arthur Treacher	555
	Orange Julius	505
Pancake houses	International House of Pancakes	419
Family-style restaurants	Big Boy	903
	Hardees	782
	Bonanza	710
	Long John Silver's	480
Dinner-style restaurants	The Peddlar	37
	Love's World Pit Barbecue	31
Delicatessen restaurants	Big Top Deli	64
	Bagel Nosh	50

Source: *Entrepreneur* Magazine, March 1980, pp. 21–54.

reheating at home—is one of the tactics they are using. Some outlets have even installed gasoline pumps in an attempt to draw more customers into their stores.

Both the number of franchised units and total sales increased appreciably in 1979—and this growth is expected to continue in the near future, particularly in smaller towns and suburban areas. In 1979, the largest franchisors and the number of franchised outlets were Seven-Eleven—2,680; Piggly Wiggly—1,000; and Convenience Food Mart—900.

Food Retailing Other Than Convenience Stores

Included in this category are doughnut shops; sellers of ice cream, yogurt, and desserts; and specialty stores offering such items as cheese, snack foods, gourmet foods, candy, fruits and nuts, and wines.

Together, these outlets rang up sales of 3.6 billion dollars in 1978. The doughnut and ice cream shops are by far the most important in this category, and the largest franchisors are well established. Some of the larger ones, and the number of outlets they reported in 1979, are

Energizing the Economy

*Ben Franklin stores:
the turn of the century
and today.*

Dairy Queen—4,850; Baskin Robbins—2,411; Carvel—750; Dunkin Donuts—980; Mister Donut—805; and Paradise Donut Shops—300. Among the specialty stores, Hickory Farms of Ohio was the largest, with 435 franchised outlets.

Nonfood Merchandising

This category embraces many products, including general merchandise, cosmetics, home furnishings, drugs, and wearing apparel. Catalogue sales houses belong to this group, and Montgomery Ward franchised sales outlets totaled 1,395 in 1979. One of the best known general merchandise franchisors is Ben Franklin Stores, a division of City Products Corporation, which currently franchises stores in all fifty states plus the Territory of Guam. With almost 2,000 stores and over fifty years of franchising experience, Ben Franklin offers franchisees a fine-tuned, time-tested program averaging around 10 percent pretax return on sales and a pretax return on investment of 25 percent.

The success of Ben Franklin and its franchised operators is attributable to two factors:

1. A highly trained group of buying/merchandising specialists operating in the headquarters offices in Des Plaines, Illinois.

2. A variety of services available to franchisees, enabling the independent store owner to match competition both in operating techniques and in attracting consumers.

Beginning with site selection and the search for prospective owners, Ben Franklin marketing and real estate experts carefully research areas and screen people to assure compatibility with the Ben Franklin

program. The belief that people are the keys to successful store operations is important, as shown by the care taken to "fit" the prospect to the store, the community, and the local clientele.

A professional staff of over 150 field operations personnel continually work with store owners and managers, advising and counseling. Latest merchandising trends and techniques are blended with the most efficient operation systems to give each store operator every known advantage in financial control, personnel selection and training, inventory management, merchandise mix, display and promotion, advertising, and store fixturing.

A headquarters staff cooperates in the development of annual sales programs incorporating advertising/promotional opportunities with fashion and product trends. The independent store operator has the option to use all of the program or such portions that suit his needs. Each promotional offering has many options to accommodate different store sizes, geographic and climatic requirements, and individual store merchandise stocks. Owners, however, have the option to purchase elsewhere, and to promote on their own or with others.[3]

Goodyear Tire and Rubber has 1,750 outlets, but only 20 percent of these are franchises rather than company-owned.

In 1979, sales in this category came to 9.6 billion dollars and are expected to increase to 10.6 billion in 1980. During the same period, the number of outlets are expected to climb by 10 percent, from 36,287 to 39,951.

The variety store remains an attractive investment for retail-oriented businessmen.

Auto Products and Services

If you own a car in need of even minor repair, the chances are that you dread taking it to your friendly neighborhood garage or dealer. What used to be an easily affordable expense no longer is. An itemized bill will usually list labor charges far exceeding the cost of parts. The solution: Fix it yourself. It's not that difficult to change a spark plug, oil filter or air filter, or to tighten a fan belt. Inflation has bred a new army of self-styled home mechanics—and with it, a booming business, not just in auto parts, but also in tools. Not only have most of the company-owned discount department store outlets opened auto parts departments, but there has also been a concomitant increase in the number of franchised auto parts outlets. The tire companies are the biggest of these, but they also sell accessories and parts in addition to tires. Some also offer repair services.

Aggressive franchisors have also been developing franchise systems to perform the more complicated repairs that few car owners are capable of. They specialize in lubrication, tune-ups, rustproofing, painting, the installation of mufflers and tailpipes, and transmission repair, as well as, for convenience, automatic car washes.

Sales for 1980 in this products/services group are being estimated at 8.3 billion dollars, with tire outlets accounting for over a third of the total.

There are some very large franchisors in this group. Some of the largest—and the number of outlets reported in 1979—are

Parts, Inc.	565
Midas Muffler	1007
Scottie Muffler	540
Nanna Carwash	4700
Ziebart Rustproofing	750
Tuff-Cote Dinal	500
Rochemco	650
Tidy Car	2100
Mechanical Man Car Wash Factory	1059
Aamco Transmissions	829

In addition to these, Goodyear Tire and Rubber reported 1,750 outlets in 1979, but 1,400 of these were company-owned.

Leisure and Travel Business

Shorter work weeks, longer vacations, increased number of holidays and days off, rising personal income, earlier retirement, have all contributed to the success story in this area, which includes hotels and motels, and a variety of entertainment, recreation, and travel businesses. With sales estimated at 6.7 billion dollars in 1979, franchisors expect an 11 percent increase in 1980, to an estimated 7.4 billion. The number of establishments is also expected to increase from 10,170 in 1979 to 10,751 the following year.

Hotels and Motels   Mid-1979 found the industry in a period of uncertainty, as high food prices, both on and off the road, increasing labor costs, spiraling fuel costs, and localized gasoline shortages took their toll. It was a mixed picture, however, with downtown hotels and airport motels holding their own while interstate motels were feeling the energy pinch. For all hotels and motels in 1979, the average occupancy rate—the major indicator of the lodging industry's economic health—is estimated at more than 73 percent, about 2 percentage points above the 1978 rate. Hotel and motel franchisors in 1979 represented 5,544 establishments, with receipts estimated at 6.3 billion dollars. Survey respondents expect that receipts will rise by 11 percent in 1980, to an estimated 7 billion dollars.

Campgrounds   The back-to-nature movement—particularly among younger people—and rising vacation costs in an inflationary environment have led to an upsurge in camping.

Franchised campgrounds numbered 990 in 1979, with estimated sales of 115 million dollars. Receipts are expected to increase about 3 percent in 1980, to 119 million.

Recreation, Entertainment, and Travel   Franchising firms that are engaged in the recreation, entertainment, and travel business report estimated sales of 273 million dollars in 1979, compared with 291 million in 1978. Sales in 1980 are expected to climb to 309 million dollars, a jump of almost 14 percent over 1979.

Travel and leisure have been rapid-growth industries in the past two decades, and Holiday Inns and Playboy Enterprises have been leaders.

The Playboy Club

Energizing the Economy

Business and Personal Services

A whole array of both personal and business services has been franchised. Small businesses, in particular, can cut equipment and personnel costs by utilizing these services. There is more paperwork than ever, and a deluge of forms and documents need to be copied. Equipment rental can cut down on capital expenditures, and the availability of franchised specialists reduces employee costs.

Business Aids and Services The increasing complexity of our tax laws has not only confused many people, but has made them determined to "beat the I.R.S"—or at least take advantage of every loophole. This attitude has helped H. & R. Block to develop a franchise system of a reported 4,399 units in 1979. In addition, the firm had 4,046 company-owned units in the same year. General Business Services, which specializes in tax, accounting, and financial services, reported 998 franchisees. Five other franchisors providing similar services claimed from 100 to 350 units.

Small businesses require advertising to bring in the customers and ring up sales. Getting To Know You (GTKY) is a franchisor in this type of service.

GTKY is in the new homeowner welcome business. It is a publisher and prepares telephone directories for local communities, which it then distributes to new homeowners in those communities shortly after they move in. There is no cost to the homeowner for the directory. GTKY solicits sponsors to pay for this program from among local merchants, professionals, and service companies. GTKY operates a business of this type in over 950 communities in the states of Massachusetts, Connecticut, New York, New Jersey, Pennsylvania, Delaware, and Maryland. It also franchises similar businesses in other states. GTKY has been in operation since 1962. The business was founded by Irving Siegel, who is still actively involved as president of the company. Other officers have been with the company since 1966. The franchisees can rely on a thoroughly experienced back-up organization.

This is a noncomplex business for the franchisee, because the parent company provides the complete support operations he requires. The franchisee is solely concerned with soliciting sponsors in his territory (which comprises ten or more suburban communities), delivering directories, and collecting payment from sponsors each month. The parent company provides editorial, art, and typography services, prints the directories, and provides all supplies required, at the request of the franchisee. In addition, the parent company offers a continuing total guidance, service, and support program for every need of the franchisee.

Although one GTKY franchise can serve a Standard Metropolitan Statistical Area (SMSA), it can be successfully operated in a unit as small as one employee, the owner, and some part-time help for clerical and shipping work. The largest SMSA franchises would require six or seven persons, one or two in the office, the rest in field sales. One salesperson usually services eight to twelve communities a year. The franchise owner should be both the sales manager and the general manager of the franchised operation.

It takes about one year for a one-person franchise to develop. The average year-old small franchise derives income from 125 to 250 sponsors, each paying about $375 per year. A franchise with more employees during development will develop faster, but attendant additional costs will keep profit at a very similar level. (See Table 2–1 for profit and cash flow projections for a one-person franchise.)

The initial franchise fee is $16,000, and it must be paid in full prior to the start of training. In addition, there is a royalty payment that averages about $45 per month for each community served; this royalty varies with the number of sponsors in each community.

During the development of a small GTKY franchise, the franchisee will need at least $8,000 in operating capital and cash reserve, and a car. If the franchisee desires to develop the business at a faster rate, with more employees, an additional investment in operating capital of about $5,000 per employee would be needed. As is apparent in the cash flow table, the business does not produce profit for almost a year, so the franchisee must also have money to live on during that period.

The parent company provides a complete training program which includes one week in the home office training school, followed shortly thereafter by one week of field training in the franchisee's territory. Several months later, there is an additional two-day field seminar in the techniques required for renewal of the sponsors. This training, home office, and field support are included in the initial franchise fee. In addition to being trained personally, the franchisee may send her or his newly recruited sales representatives to home office training schools during any of the six annual sales training cycles. There is no charge to the franchisee for tuition and textbooks for these employees; however, their transportation, meals, and lodging for the minimum three-day session must be paid. The parent company recommends that all sales representatives attend home office training schools, where most graduates receive the training necessary to achieve a high rate of success, but there is no requirement that the reps be sent to this school, and they may be trained in their own area. The parent company will send a field sales manager to the franchisee's territory, at the latter's request, to provide field sales training for employees. Travel, lodging, meals, and a per diem fee are paid by the franchisee for this parent company service.

The parent company sponsors several meetings every year, usually at the home office, which are open to all franchisees and their sales reps. The parent company sends a regular monthly newsletter to the franchisees, giving them information about the company, the sales programs, and various other important items. From time to time, bulletins are sent out on urgent topics. The parent company maintains toll-free WATS lines for communication with franchisees at all times.

The cash flow and profit projection on the previous pages indicates the cash position at the end of one and two years of operations, with a single salesperson working the franchise. At the end of one year, it is projected that seven editions will be in print. By the end of the second year, eleven editions should be in print, and six of these editions will already have gone through their first renewal in stages. The staging of initial and renewal sales is indicated on the top line of the projection above the month number. The next line indicating month numbers starts as soon as the franchisee returns to his or her territory and completes field training.

1. We assume an average sale of twenty-two sponsors per edition at an average of thirty-five distributions per month. Calculating a sale at $1.25 per distribution per sponsor, with a small allowance for bad debts, we project, on first editions, an income of $950 per month per

Table 2-1

GTKY Cash Flow and Profit Projection—One Salesperson

Note: This is a wide spreadsheet. Column groups are: Months 1–12, a 12-Month Totals column, Months 13–24, a second 12-Month Totals column, a 2-Year Totals column, and an "Av. 2nd Yr % of Sales" column. The header band "Books Published (#) or Renewed (R)" carries the edition indices 1–11 and renewal indices R1–R6.

Item	M1	M2	M3	M4	M5	M6	M7	M8	M9	M10	M11	M12	12-Mo Totals	M13	M14	M15	M16	M17	M18	M19	M20	M21	M22	M23	M24	12-Mo Totals	2-Year Totals	Av. 2nd Yr % of Sales
Books Published (#) or Renewed (R)	1	2	3	4	5	6							7		R1	8	R2	R3	9		10	R4	R5		R6	11		
INCOME																												
From first edition sponsors	800	950	950	1,900	1,900	2,850	2,850	3,800	4,750	4,750	5,700	5,700	30,400	6,650	6,650	5,700	5,700	6,650	6,650	7,600	6,650	5,700	5,700	5,700	6,650	76,000		
Renewed sponsors														1,050	1,050	2,100	3,250	3,250	3,250	3,250	4,300	5,450	5,450	6,500		38,900		
Total	800	950	950	1,900	1,900	2,850	2,850	3,800	4,750	4,750	5,700	5,700	30,400	7,700	7,700	7,800	8,950	9,900	9,900	10,850	10,950	11,150	11,150	12,200	6,650	114,900	145,300	
EXPENSES																												
Address book purchases	800	800	800	800	800	800	800	800	800	800	800	800	9,600	1,600	1,600	1,600	1,600	1,600	1,600	1,600	1,600	1,600	1,600			16,000	25,600	14
Royalties													1,440													5,010	6,450	4.3
Sales Expenses													8,750													13,400	22,150	11.6
Postage													315													900	1,215	.8
Telephone													460													750	1,210	.7
Insurance													1,000													1,000	2,000	.8
Automobile Expense	300	300	300	300	300	300	300	300	300	300	300	300	3,600	300	300	300	300	300	300	300	300	300	300	300	300	3,600	7,200	3.1
Book Delivery													1,365													3,850	5,215	3.3
Office Supplies													550													1,200	1,750	1
Clerical Help													1,950													6,950	8,900	6
Misc.													640													1,025	1,665	.9
Total													29,670													53,615	83,285	45.7
PROFIT OR (LOSS) EACH MONTH	(880)	(1,625)	(880)	440	(1,710)	(570)	425	(85)	405	260	2,050	2,900	730	2,405	3,265	3,010	3,125	4,320	7,120	4,630	5,655	6,600	8,035	5,985	7,135	61,285		53.3
CASH FLOW	(880)	(2,505)	(3,385)	(2,945)	(4,655)	(5,225)	(4,800)	(4,885)	(4,480)	(4,220)	(2,170)	730	730	3,135	6,400	9,410	12,535	16,855	23,975	28,605	34,260	40,860	48,895	54,880	62,015	62,015	62,015	99.0

edition. ($1.25 x 22 x 35). The income starts to be collected the month after the edition is published, and then continues, for purposes of this projection, at a uniform rate until renewal.

2. Renewal editions are calculated on a similar basis; however, experience has shown that the average renewal rate grows. Therefore, we have increased income from renewal editions by $100, to reflect slightly more than a 10-percent increase.

3. Sales expense for original editions is figured at $1250 as commission and car allowance for a sales representative. If the sales are made by the franchisee himself, the sales commissions would then, of course, be paid to him.

4. On renewals, sales expense is increased to reflect the greater number of subscribers.

5. Automobile expenses indicated here are to be paid only to the franchise owner. Automobile expenses to commission-sales reps would be covered in their commissions.

6. Except for month one, when basic office tools may be needed, the franchisee receives supplies from the parent company adequate for about six months. Thereafter, supplies are purchased both locally and from the home office as needed. These purchases include the follow-up program and other items at estimated costs.

7. At the start of the franchise operation, only a small amount of part-time clerical help is required for the distribution, collating, packing, shipping, and billing. As the franchise grows, the requirements for part-time help increase proportionately to volume.

8. At some point during the second year, the part-time help will have to be replaced by a full-time clerk.

The percentages calculated in the last column of the projection are fairly stable, no matter how large the operation grows.

The concept of real estate franchising has developed into the fastest growing sector of the franchising system. Combined with a strong demand for houses—both for owner occupancy and for investment—and with higher prices, franchised real estate brokers amassed 4.1 billion dollars in gross commissions in 1979; these are expected to rise to 5.6 billion in 1980. The number of outlets should show great strength, jumping from 24,389 in 1979 to 33,733 in 1980.

Century 21 Real Estate, in business since 1972, has over 7,000 franchises in fifty states. The franchisee must be a qualified real estate broker with a good track record in the industry. In effect, he or she must be able to run a real estate brokerage operation.

Snelling and Snelling, an employment agency, had 670 franchised offices in 1979, and two other systems reported over 200. Manpower, the temporary personnel service, had 454 franchisees in 1979 and 279 company-owned offices.

Franchised outlets engaged in the printing and copying services produced sales of more than 285 million dollars in 1979. Almost 34 percent of the 2,362 outlets reported for 1978 were located in three states—California, Texas, and Florida. Alert to new and potential business opportunities, franchisors in printing and copying services have catered to the printing needs of a variety of small organizations such as associations, clubs and societies, retail outlets, wholesalers, job-

Among the most recent industries to franchise was real estate, but in less than ten years Century 21 has grown to more than 7,000 outlets.

bers, and distributors. The outlook for continued expansion in this area is extremely bright, with sales expected to reach 337 million dollars in 1980, while the number of outlets should advance to 3,313.

Construction, Home Improvement, and Cleaning Service Homes, offices, plants, and institutions provide a large market for the cleaning of carpeting and upholstery. Duraclean, a firm specializing in such services, reported 1,200 franchisees in 1979.

Water conditioning is another service belonging to this category. Water Refining claimed 1,074 franchisees in 1979, and Culligan Water Conditioners, 903.

Lawn care, furniture refinishing and repair, pavement and driveway repair, and even swimming pool construction are businesses that have been franchised. In all, there were over 14,000 franchised establishments in these fields in 1978, with sales of an estimated 1.2 billion dollars.

Equipment Rentals Need a rototiller or a sandblaster? It's expensive, and if you plan to use it only once, or infrequently, why make an investment when you can rent it? You don't have to worry about maintenance or repair—and when you've finished the job, it goes back to the rental company instead of taking up valuable storage space.

There are lots of people—and businesses—that find it convenient and economical to rent party supplies, gardening equipment, light construction equipment, among others on a long list of infrequently needed items. In 1978, there were some 1,488 franchised rental outlets—with estimated sales of 212 million dollars—to provide them.

Taylor Rental, which supplies tools and related equipment, claimed 624 franchisees in 1979. To show that almost anything can be rented, a firm by the name of Port-o-let Company had 28 franchisees in the same year. What does it rent? Portable toilets.

Educational Services   Businesses engaged in franchising educational services have carried specialization to the nth degree. Franchised schools exist in the fields of modeling, speedreading, acting, personal improvement, auto and truck driving, diet and exercise, computer operation, and secretarial skills. Even day nurseries have become franchised. There were over 2,200 franchised units in this category in 1978, with estimated sales of 272 million dollars.

In 1979, the John Robert Powers modeling school had 70 franchised outlets. Barbizon International, which is in modeling, fashion, and acting, claimed 80 franchisees in the same year. Other educational franchisors (and the number of franchisees in 1979) are: Mary Moppet's Day Care Schools, 77; Image of Loveliness (personal improvement courses), 75. These are some of the largest; there are many others.

Haircutting, which accounted for over 10 billion dollars in retail business last year, has fast shaped up to be one of the most lucrative franchise investment opportunities.

Heading the field is Command Performance—a worldwide chain that has applied the success formula developed in the fast-food field to the current trend toward natural, easy-to-care-for hairstyling for both men and women.

Since its 1976 inception, Command Performance has opened more than 480 salons throughout the United States, including Puerto Rico and Hawaii, Canada and Costa Rica. Richard J. Wall, chairman and cofounder of Command Performance, attributes the success of this personal service retail operation to several policies common to McDonald's, Burger King, and other well-known franchise operations.

A carefully designed, well-planned operation. The owner is given detailed assistance in all phases of running the business from bookkeeping to the selection of equipment.
Identical store design and atmosphere—bright, bold and different from the traditional barber shop or beauty salon—to capture the mood and lifestyle of the 16 to 40 age group (the target customer for Command Performance).
Consistent, high-quality customer service. Command Performance hires and trains the staff for each salon and provides its hairstylists with frequent advanced educational sessions. Command Performance's three-man team of styling experts conduct both in-store training as well as teach advanced courses at the Command Performance International Centre for Advanced Hair Design.

According to Mr. Wall, the franchise is designed as an investment opportunity with a high rate of return and semiabsentee ownership. Previous experience in the hairstyling or beauty industry is, surprisingly enough, not necessary and even discouraged. "We prefer our own proven methods of operation," says Wall.

A cross section of Command Performance owners ranges from commercial airplane pilot to CPA, professor to police officer, corporate CEO to farmer, retired army colonel to car dealer.

"Command Performance is the store owner's partner," states Wall.

Energizing the Economy

The franchise package is a virtual turnkey operation that includes ongoing support.

A typical Command Performance hairstyling salon, measuring 1,500 square feet and with twelve styling stations, is located in an easily accessible shopping center or mall in key traffic areas.

Currently, Command Performance salons expect weekly business receipts to average between $5,000 and $6,500, with some reporting over $15,000 per week. Operating results show that investors also achieve a highly attractive (20 to 30 percent) pretax return. Annual gross sales range from $260,000 to $700,000, with yearly breakeven (including debt service) usually running between $137,000 and $195,000.

"The Command Performance hairstyling salon," says Wall, "is for the person who wants to own a successful business and be a part of the newest opportunity for growth."[4]

Laundry and Dry-Cleaning Service Although new fabrics and improved home laundering equipment have caused some problems for those service businesses, continued growth is expected due to addition of such services as drapery processing, rental of rug-cleaning equipment, and alteration work.

There were over 2,900 franchised laundry and dry-cleaning outlets in 1978 which reported sales of 256 million dollars.

Auto and Truck Rental Services Franchisors in this business are attempting to meet rising fuel and vehicle prices by using more fuel-efficient cars and by improving maintenance systems to stretch out the useful life of their vehicles. Hertz and National Car Rental System are no longer franchising.[5] Sales in 1978 were estimated at 2.3 billion dollars.

International Markets for Franchising

You probably expect to find some of America's best-known fast-food restaurants north of the border in Canada. However, if you're planning a trip to England or to Europe, you'll find them there, too. Even the Japanese have taken to American fast food and doughnuts.

Summary and Conclusion.

If you were to ask what shape the American economy would be in today *without* franchising, you would be asking a perfectly justifiable question.

To say that franchising's impact on the U.S. economy has been significant would be a gross understatement. The hard statistics for 1980 tell the story: an estimated 338 billion dollars in sales; 488,000 franchised outlets; over 4 million employees.

The traditional types of franchises, the automobile dealerships, the gasoline stations, and the soft-drink bottlers, have been with us for a long time. Traditional franchising still dominates the franchising field in terms of sales, and it is estimated that it will account for about 75 percent of total 1980 franchise sales volume. The number of establishments, however, is expected to decline in the 1980s, mainly due to closings of gasoline stations and mergers of existing franchised bottling plants.

It is the newer types of franchises, the entire business format or trademark/trade name systems, that have virtually exploded onto the American scene, particularly since the 1950s. While the number of

American franchisors have been quick to realize the overseas opportunities for their products. Homesick travelers can now find McDonald's golden arches on every continent. Pictured is a Tokyo outlet.

Chart 2-4
International Food Franchising in 1978

Franchising Companies 266
Number of franchising outlets 17,156

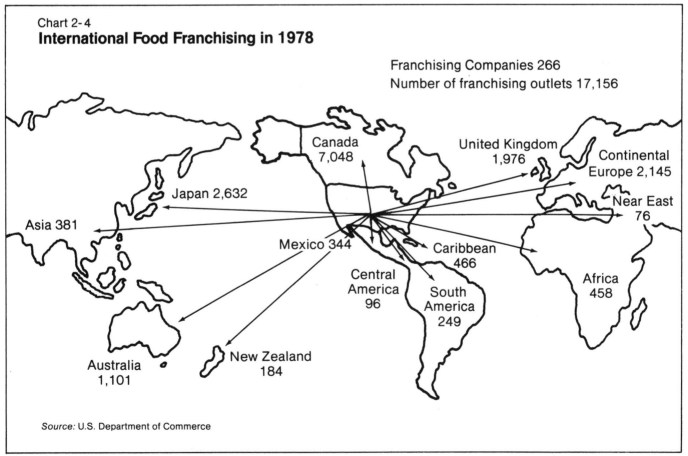

Canada 7,048
United Kingdom 1,976
Continental Europe 2,145
Japan 2,632
Asia 381
Near East 76
Mexico 344
Caribbean 466
Central America 96
South America 249
Africa 458
Australia 1,101
New Zealand 184

Source: U.S. Department of Commerce

traditional franchised outlets declined to about 191,380 in 1980, the number of entire business format outlets stood at approximately 297,000 in the same year.

The stars of this new type of franchising have been the fast-food restaurants. In 1977, there were almost 52,000 fast-food franchised outlets, employing over 1,230,000 people.

The most important segment of franchising is retailing. In 1979, retailing accounted for about 90 percent of total franchise sales but, more importantly, for about one-third of total retail sales in the United States.

Almost any type of business, it seems, can be franchised. While retailing dominates the franchise field, service businesses have also been franchised, and there is every indication that there will be continued growth in this area.

Much of the success of franchising, particularly within the entire business format systems, is attributable to modern management, merchandising, and advertising techniques. Without these tools, it is doubtful that these outlets could have contributed as much to the American economy—if indeed, many of them would have existed at all. Much of this advanced management system, although by no means all, has been provided by some of America's largest corporations, which have been acquiring franchisors as part of their diversification programs.

In what shape would the American economy be today without franchising? It is known that the rate of business failure is much lower among franchised businesses than among nonfranchised ones. So, today, there are probably over half a million independently owned franchised outlets, employing well over 4 million people.

Through the payment of salaries and wages, franchising has contributed greatly to the total purchasing power of the nation. This purchasing power has, in turn, helped to sustain many other businesses. These employees all pay taxes, too, and both the franchisors and franchisees pay federal, state, and local business taxes in addition to contributing to social security funds.

Certainly franchising's contribution to the American economy has been more than significant. Even more important, to many ambitious people, franchising has provided the answer to the American dream of owning one's own business.

The Advantages and Disadvantages of Franchising

The Alternatives

Why should you become a franchisee? If you want to go into business for yourself, there are many ways to do it other than by signing an agreement with a franchisor. You can certainly just start your own business. Start-up costs will be involved; you'll have to work harder than ever, and if you've been a salaried employee for someone else, you'll have to get along without that regular paycheck. But many successful businesses have been started just this way.

You could also buy a business from someone else. That might be an advantage over starting from scratch because you're buying a recognized firm, respected by those already doing business with it.

If you already own a business and are considering expanding, why franchise? There are other ways to expand. You could try convincing

There are alternatives to franchising, which you should look into before you make your move.

The Advantages and Disadvantages of Franchising

other independent outlets to take on your line of products or services. You might convince people in other markets to start up new businesses to market your products. Or you could open other company-owned branches staffed by company employees.

Other alternatives to franchising are voluntary chain organizations. Here are two examples:

Independent Grocers Alliance (I.G.A.). They collect dues and have membership contracts. They stock national brands, plus their own private brands. Management merchandising, advertising, and promotional assistance are available. Accounting, store layout, and sales clerk training are also a part of the services supplied to members.

The True Value Hardware trademark is owned by Cotter and Company, a mutual wholesale organization. It was formed in 1947 and is entirely owned by the retail dealers. Dealers buy an equal amount of voting stock, thus giving them an equal voice in controlling overall policy. The company provides a complete package of advertising, merchandising, and promotional materials to stores requesting all or part of the package. Trade shows are held for the members, and purchasing is done from catalogues. Though it is not mandatory to purchase all merchandising through Cotter, the individual dealers' interests are best served by buying from their own company. Net profits of Cotter are distributed to the members in the form of dividends. Ace Hardware has a similar plan for its members.

The franchise system, however, is as viable an option as the others. It too has its advantages and its disadvantages to both franchisors and franchisees. That's why it's wise to look at each separately.

It takes money to expand—and those running a business might not wish to sell stock or pledge its assets against a loan. Even with a good credit rating, the amount of capital required might be so large as to

True Value Hardware is an interesting example of one of the alternatives to franchising: a mutual wholesale organization.

make securing the needed funds difficult. "If the parent firm's choice is between expansion through franchising or no expansion at all, the franchising route can provide income that otherwise would not be present—income from franchise sales and royalties."[1]

One of the most dramatic examples of the effective use of capital raised through franchises is the case of John Y. Brown, Jr., the current governor of Kentucky and the former owner and president of Kentucky Fried Chicken. Brown borrowed and invested 2 million dollars in the chicken business in 1963. In 1971, he sold out for a 35-million-dollar profit. Mr. Brown has stated that it would have required 450 million dollars for his company to have established its first 2,700 stores. This sum was not available to him when he started his business, but franchisee-provided capital gave him the funds to make the expansion possible.[2]

Even if the expanding firm could raise the necessary capital by other means, there are other advantages to raising such capital by selling franchises. The capital is interest-free and there are generally few, if any, restrictions on how these funds can be spent.

Time is another factor. Franchises can usually be offered quite quickly, subject to the laws of the states in which they are to be sold. On the other hand, a company can't make a decision to sell stock on one day and have it offered to the public the next. There are regulatory procedures to be followed that are time-consuming. Borrowing takes time, too.

In raising capital, the franchisor should not expect to depend entirely on the franchisee's money for the finance that will put him in the franchise business. Nor should the franchisor use the franchisee's money as risk venture capital to experiment with an idea, which, if it proves not to be workable, would leave the franchisee high and dry

Sanders Court in the 1930s where the Colonel developed his Finger Lickin' Good chicken recipe. When a new interstate highway bypassed his establishment in Corbin, Kentucky, Colonel Sanders took to the road to sell his franchised method.

SANDERS COURT & CAFE
CORBIN ——— KENTUCKY

Corbin, Ky.
Junct. U. S. 25, 25E and 25W
32 Rooms — 32 Baths
At Asheville, N. C.
5 Miles North
At Junct. U. S. 25, 70, 19 and 23

The Advantages and Disadvantages of Franchising

because the franchisor—in this instance, truly a promotor—has merely invested seed capital to seek out prospective franchisees.

When such a situation occurs, the undercapitalized promoter—not by my definition a franchisor—cannot secure the franchisee's investment, but must, like the Ponzi scheme of old, use subsequent deposits to meet prior financial obligations. Can this still happen in the year of 1980? Read the following FTC news summary.

**FTC Alleges Fraud, Wins Court Order
Freezing Assets of "Hot Box" Pizza;
Nearly Two Million Dollars at Stake**

At least 60 investors have each been defrauded of as much as $100,000, in some cases their life savings, by a company selling worthless frozen-pizza distributorships, the Federal Trade Commission charged in a complaint made public today.

The total lost by investors to H. N. Singer, Inc. for its "Hot Box Products" business may approach $2 million, the FTC's San Francisco Regional Office estimates.

The complaint was filed in U.S. District Court in San Francisco against the Chicago-based company and four individuals who allegedly control it. The Commission is seeking restitution for customers' losses and a permanent injunction against the challenged practices.

The FTC meanwhile obtained a temporary restraining order from the court, freezing the assets of Singer and the four individuals and prohibiting violations of the FTC trade-regulation rule on franchising and business-opportunity ventures. In seeking the order, the Commission argued that since the company's officials have been known to establish other fraudulent schemes, then move and assume aliases to escape prosecution, the assets had to be frozen to ensure that funds would be available for possible investor restitution.

Singer is charged with violating the FTC franchising and business-opportunity rule by failing to disclose the true nature of the business it was offering. This is the first enforcement case under the 1979 rule.

Lured by newspaper-ad promises of "You Fly, We Pay" for sales-briefing trips and the prospect of "$100,000 Per Year and More," the investors allegedly paid $25,000 for the right to sell Hot Box Products-brand frozen pizza to establishments such as bars and bowling alleys.

These retail accounts were to be secured in advance by Hot Box Products representatives, according to the FTC complaint, and the company's sales literature also promised "17 vital aids to success," which included "full company assistance and guidance, complete company training, dealer manual, 'point-of-sale' promotional materials, operating records, bookkeeping and accounting systems, accounts efficiently and systematically established in your area, protected geographical area. . . ."

The complaint charges that while most of the distributors did eventually receive shipments of frozen pizza and the "Hot Box Products ovens" in which they were to be heated (though .usually after several months' delay), little, if any of the promised company support was forthcoming.

As for the "secured retail accounts" where the pizza was to be cooked and eaten, the complaint further charges that most turned out to worthless. The majority allegedly purchased few, if any, pizzas, with many often lacking sufficient freezer space for the products.

Investigators found cases where the signatures of retail owners were allegedly forged on Hot Box Products account agreements.

"Within a short period of time [after] starting operations," the complaint claims, "most Hot Box Products franchisees were faced with continuing freezer expenses for frozen-pizza storage and very few viable retail accounts to which to sell the pizzas."

The FTC franchising and business-opportunity rule requires that, before signing an agreement, prospective investors be given detailed and accurate information on the earnings they can reasonably expect, the costs they will incur, the company's history and financial standing, as well as other aspects of the venture. In most of these areas, the complaint says, Singer's disclosures were either lacking or false.

Misrepresentations were charged concerning the cost and availability of freezer space, the availability of training, the company's stability and many other circumstances surrounding Hot Box Products distributorships.

Copies of the FTC complaint against H. N. Singer, Inc. are available from the Public Reference Branch, Room 130, FTC, Sixth Street and Pennsylvania Avenue N.W., Washington, D.C. 20580; (202) 523-3598. Vol. 43-80, 7/30/80 (File No. 802-3146)

Motivation is one of the keys to success in franchising. Motivation means many different things to people, but in franchising it means the right physical and mental state that pushes individuals to act in a positive manner or they stand to lose their hard-earned savings. Yes, the fear of losing money is a big motivator. The franchisee is not a salaried employee, he's a businessman intent on making money—for himself. He's not going to maximize his income without a concerted effort. He's also got a financial stake in the business and is unlikely to walk away from it and lose his investment.

Raising capital quickly and acquiring dedicated people to market a franchisor's products or services are the major advantages of franchising to a business wishing to expand. But there are others.

With a sufficient number of franchised outlets, the franchisor can take advantage of quantity discounts on many of the items needed in running the system, thus providing the opportunity for larger profits.

Local ownership of an outlet is frequently an advantage, too. Local zoning boards are often involved in granting certificates of occupancy. Residents may not want some purple and orange building in their town, particularly one with a big parking lot frequented by loiterers with nothing better to do. But a local resident known by the townspeople is much more likely to receive favorable consideration than is some outsider.

Labor relations should prove less difficult. Unions would find it far more difficult to deal with many individual franchisees than with one central office of a company with its own outlets.

Like the producers of petroleum products in the 1930s, franchising also allows the franchisor more flexibility in meeting local market conditions than can a company which imposes policy from some distant central office, as is the case with company-owned outlets.

Disadvantages to Franchisor

Making a franchise system work requires good, capable people as franchisees. Such people are not always easy to find. They have to have at least a little business ability and a willingness to expend the effort required to make the franchise successful. They should be willing to be trained and not be so independent as to ignore company policies and procedures. A franchise satisfied with a less than average income is not likely to devote the time and energy necessary to return a satisfactory level of income to the franchisor.

On the other hand, if a franchisee is extremely successful, she or he might eventually come to resent paying royalty fees and the other contributions agreed to in the franchise contract.

The Advantages and Disadvantages of Franchising

A franchisor is bound to exercise less control over a franchisee than over an employee. Harry Winokur, president of Mr. Donut, compares franchisees to underdeveloped countries. He says, "They accept aid but resent it."[3]

Franchising clearly offers a dynamic and powerful method to build an effective distribution network without depleting a company's capital. In addition, franchisees tend to be more highly motivated than salaried employees. On the other hand, there are problems in dealing with people who are not employees. Litigation is a possibility and so is the problem of finding qualified franchisees. Perry Mendel, president of Kinder-Care Learning Centers, a child day-care chain, discussed some of the problems in an interview with *Forbes* magazine:

"Right from the start I expected it to be big, like Holiday Inns. I would not have gone into it unless I thought I would have an opportunity to accomplish the vastness of what I dreamed about."

Logically, then, the group hired a professional franchise-selling outfit called E.C.K. Chivers in Miami, Florida, who had gotten the Lums restaurant chain started. "Franchising looked like the way to raise front dollars," says Mendel. "So we ran our first ad in the Wall Street Journal: *'Join the good ship Lollipop'." Mendel scowls. "I said, What kind of ad is this? But we got a tremendous response."*

About seven months later, Mendel stopped franchising altogether. Today, he calls it "the greatest decision we ever made." He explains: "The people who thought they would love to be in the day-care business—an ex-teacher or an ex-minister who love to take care of children—knew nothing about getting a building into existence, or finance. If we were going to have to arrange for all the financing, which is no mean trick, and get just 5% of gross revenues for all this effort, it didn't make sense."[4]

Franchising has its own set of legal problems. Chase Revel, writing in the March 1980 issue of *Entrepreneur* magazine, said: "Today, the biggest headache for a franchisor is legalities. Fifteen states require a full disclosure of intimate company details to every prospective franchisee and a costly state registration. Your legal and accounting costs may run from $10,000 to $50,000 for the first state." In addition, some states have fairness doctrines, which means that, if in the opinion of the state, the franchise contract is not fair, the state has the right to issue a cease-and-desist order. In other words, the franchisor has to stop selling the franchise. Finally, in all states with franchise laws (except Virginia) the state can impound all the funds received by the franchisor from the franchisee until the franchisor has performed all the duties under the franchise agreement.[5]

Finally, not all companies can make use of the franchising method. If the product is a service, it must be able to fit this unique method of distribution.

Charles L. Vaughn, a franchise specialist, has stated:

A problem in evaluating the relative merits of franchising versus the alternatives is the lack of comparative empirical data for non-franchised businesses and even for salaried jobs. Undoubtedly, most of the negative features of franchising are present in the alternatives, and many of franchising's advantages are lacking in these alternatives. In the nonfranchised business, however, the entrepreneur is not faced with exaggerations in regard to the profits and franchisor assistance which are to be forthcoming.[6]

Advantages to the Franchisee

Respected Trade Name All other things being equal, wouldn't you rather open a fast-food restaurant with a name like McDonald's instead of Joe Gumbash Fast Food. Of course you would. No one ever heard of Joe Gumbash Fast Food, but McDonald's is a nationally recognized, respected name. People know what to expect from a McDonald's. They know the menu, the quality of product and service, and the prices. McDonald's colors, architecture, and signs are instantly recognized. As soon as the paint dries and you open for business you can expect to attract a ready-made group of customers. It could take months, perhaps even a year to develop such a loyal following, even with an exceptionally good product at reasonable prices.

Another advantage to opening under an accepted name is that you incur no legal costs in developing your own trade name. In registering a trade name, a legal search must be conducted to ensure that no other company is using the name you might have selected. If that name is already registered, you must select a new name and start the process all over again. Such a process can not only prove to be expensive, but also time consuming.

Tested Product or Service If you join an established franchise system, you're not going to have to open a business and find out, through trial and error, whether or not your product is acceptable. The franchisor has already done that. The franchisor has done the market research, has tested the product, and has learned how to present it to the public. And the franchisor will continue to conduct such research on your behalf.

Financial Aid Many franchisors will provide varying forms of financial assistance to help you start your business. This can include loans for equipment purchase, opening inventory, or for other purposes at competitive interest rates. If not, the franchisor may have an arrangement with a nearby bank which will advance funds to a qualified franchisee prospect, again at competitive interest rates. Any financial institution will be more inclined to finance a business in a franchise system with good management and a record of success. Or the franchisor may help in arranging for the leasing of equipment or property.

A Disciplined System Many franchisors have developed complete management systems which enable the new franchisee to operate efficiently. This can include not only product preparation, as in a restaurant, but also a money-saving method of providing service. Management methods in inventory control, purchasing, bookkeeping, payroll, and, in general, successfully running a small business may all be part of the package you receive as a franchisee.

Continuing Guidance The better franchisors who provide such management systems are computerized. So, as you provide information to the franchisor by the prescribed methods, it will be fed into a computer, which will provide statistical analyses not only of your business but of all the franchisees in the system, both individually and collectively. The franchisor's staff can interpret these analyses and point out to each franchisee where her or his business is strong or weak, and what adjustments should be made to improve the operation and profit margin.

In some cases, field representatives make periodic calls on each franchisee to offer management assistance and to help in surmounting

A prime benefit to franchisees is the product recognition that comes from extensive advertising. Aamco supports its dealer outlets with an extremely effective media campaign.

some individual problem. Their intimate knowledge of other franchise operations within a specific geographical area are put to good use in providing sound advice.

Professional Advertising Campaigns   Most big franchisors charge a monthly advertising or marketing fee. In a large system with many outlets, these fees collectively can amount to millions of dollars. With this money, the franchisor can provide advertising which no individual franchisee is capable of producing. By buying advertising on a large scale, or by scheduling it on national television, the franchisor can provide advertising at a much lower cost than could a franchisee buying the same amount on a local basis.

In addition, the advertising copy, art, and television production are of the highest caliber, created by advertising professionals, backed by consumer research.

The franchisor may also provide the consumer contests, lotteries, and other promotional ideas that attract customers to the outlets.

Site Selection   That many franchisors have real estate departments has already been mentioned. Specialists in this area can use their expertise not only in selecting a favorable location, but also in negotiating lease or purchase agreements at the best possible terms.

Purchasing Power   As part of a large system, an individual franchisee is often in the position to join with other franchisees in purchasing large quantities of both required inventory and items such as stationery and other operating materials at discounts not available to an independent.

If the franchisor specifies certain suppliers, it is usually not only because quality standards will be met but also because of volume discounts which are passed along to each franchisee.

Training   Particularly to those with little management experience, the training provided by many franchisors can be of great value to the new franchisee. The trainee will learn how to handle not only delivery of the franchisor's product or service to customers but also proper small business methods. If the franchisor has a management "system," then the new franchisee will also be taught the procedures necessary to comply with that system.

One of the most successful franchise systems—McDonald's—puts every franchisee through an extensive nineteen-day training session at "Hamburger University" in Elk Grove, Illinois. The school provides detailed instruction in management decision making, particularly as it relates to running a McDonald's franchise. Kentucky Fried Chicken offers a similar training at the company's "Chicken University."[7]

The Odds for Success Are in Your Favor   The chance of succeeding in a franchise is better than in a small, independent business. Using data supplied by the Small Business Administration and other sources, J. F. Atkinson, in his booklet *Franchising: The Odds on Favorite*, shows that the risk of total failure is only one-tenth as likely for a franchise than for a nonfranchised business.[8] Furthermore, a study conducted among franchised retailers by Charles L. Vaughn revealed that an overwhelming majority of franchisees (80 percent or more) would buy the franchise again.[9]

Professional training is a valuable benefit that many franchisors offer. Industry leaders in this have been McDonald's with its Hamburger University and Kentucky Fried Chicken with its Chicken University.

The Advantages and Disadvantages of Franchising

Better Resale Value   If the franchisee, during the negotiating process, is able to insert a favorable right-to-sell clause in the franchise agreement, she or he should have a relatively easy time selling it, particularly if the business is part of a respected, well-known system. In addition, it is quite likely that the price would be higher than for a similar, nonaffiliated business.

A good franchise often sells for twice its annual earning capability, which includes both profit and the amount the franchisee takes out of the business as salary. These amounts, added to the equity in the business, provide an enviable capital gain.

Disadvantages to the Franchisee

While the advantages of a franchise seem overwhelming, some that appear to be advantages might very well turn out to be disadvantages. Much depends on the terms in the contract and how the franchisee was financed. Also, the personality of the franchisee, his or her willingness to abide by the "system," have an important bearing on the success of the business. Therefore it pays to look at a franchise from another perspective. What might be some of the disadvantages?

Designated Suppliers   The advantage of a designated supplier is supposed to be prices which reflect quantity discounts, thus giving a franchisee a competitive advantage over a nonfranchised business. But what happens if the supplier does not meet delivery schedules? Or, despite the understanding that quality control standards will be met, they are not. Suppose you find another supplier who not only can meet quality standards but can do it a price that's lower than the designated supplier's. You have no recourse if you signed an agreement which specified a supplier. You can report poor service and substandard quality, but these situations take time to correct.

Is the franchisor making money off the supplier? Kickbacks are illegal, but it can happen. If that's the case, it may be extremely difficult to correct it.

Poor Site Selection   The franchisor may insist on selecting the site for your outlet. The real estate experts, you are told, will make the best deal. But suppose the site is not a good one. An improper location can be disastrous to a retail business, particularly one that depends to a large degree on impulse visits by passing motorists. If you're on a side street with a low traffic count instead of on a heavily traveled main road, the potential of your business has been drastically reduced. Or what happens if you have a long-term lease and a new road or a bypass is built? Will the franchisor see to it that the situation is rectified? If not, you're just plain stuck. The three most important things for success in franchising are location—location—location.

An Overly Strict Management System   There's nothing wrong with a good system. If properly structured, it should make the franchisee's operation more efficient. As long as each outlet sticks to the system, particularly when dealing with customers, the public knows what to expect in each and every outlet.

It's the systems that go to extremes that can drive some franchisees to the point of rebellion. Ideas to improve the system might be rejected out-of-hand. The paperwork and the number of forms to be constantly completed may be excessive. The prospective franchisee should make sure that a franchisor's system is reasonable before signing the contract. If it is not, then the person who can't stand regimentation should think twice before making a commitment.

Long-Term Financial Commitments It may be that to obtain the funds necessary to open your business you have made many long-term financial commitments. These could include not only a bank loan, but also leases for equipment, land, and building. If, after a year or two in the business, you decide you want to sell it, you might hope to find a buyer who will assume these obligations. But if interest rates have dropped, you might not be able to sell the business at the same terms under which you financed it. Or if the economy has declined, you might have to sell at a loss, if you can afford to. If not, there you are committed to payments, with interest, for fifteen to twenty years.

Limited Ownership It is quite likely, particularly in a retailing business, that the franchisor will own the property on which your business is located, and perhaps the building too. In such a case, the franchisee agreement will undoubtedly call for a rental fee that's a percentage of gross profit. If the equipment is leased, your only physical possession may be the inventory on hand. You do own the franchise rights, for which you paid a franchise fee, but if you choose to sell the business, these rights and the operating inventory are the only things you have to sell. If the real estate has appreciated during your tenure, the owner realizes this gain, not you. You might not even be able to charge depreciation of equipment against business taxes.

Excessive and Hidden Charges Franchise fees often seem to have no economic justification. Rights to operate under a respected trademark or trade name can be very valuable, but if financing was required to pay the franchise fee, the higher the fee, the more you'll pay in interest. And royalties, rental, and marketing or advertising fees are usually a fixed percentage of gross profit. Therefore, if these payments get larger and larger, then obviously so do the profits. Everyone likes higher profits, but it can be very annoying if rental fees become grossly excessive or if you pay more for advertising than you receive. Royalty fees are supposed to cover franchisor profits and the costs of services, not advertising or rental fees.

There are often hidden charges, too. If a building needs remodeling, the franchisee may be stuck with the costs, whoever owns the building. And of course such remodeling must be done in accordance with franchisor specifications. Or there might be a fee for bookkeeping or data processing services. It is imperative that the franchisee be aware of *all* fees and charges before signing a contract.

Long Hours Some businesses, particularly restaurants, must be open for business seven days a week, often late into the evening. Others must be open six days a week. And many hours can be spent filling out forms to comply with the franchisor's dictated·procedure. It is not uncommon for some franchisees to work sixty to seventy hours a week. Don't think you're going to have a lot of free time just because you're in your own business. One of the most frequently heard complaints about franchising is the long hours required.

One-Sided Contracts It is the franchisor who writes the initial contract. Naturally, it is written with the interests of the franchisor foremost. Often thirty to forty pages in length, sometimes in small type, it is a very imposing document for the layperson to tackle, let alone understand. But it is up to the franchisee, with legal advice, to

The Advantages and Disadvantages of Franchising

make the attempt to modify the contract so as to protect his or her interests.

Sometimes there is no option to make changes in the terms, and the franchisor may be considered more of a dictator than a business partner. Under such circumstances, the franchisee might feel that she or he will not be independent, but someone bound to the franchisor by unreasonable terms.

One of these unreasonable terms may impose severe restrictions on the right of the franchisee to sell the franchise. Any businessperson likes to build equity in a business, and the inability to sell it during the life of the contract, often one of fifteen to twenty years, is a decidedly negative factor. On the other hand, the franchisor usually reserves the right to buy back the business if the franchisee is not running it according to the terms of the contract.

One student of franchising points out that clauses dealing with transfer, termination, and renewal of franchises are particularly unfair to the new, inexperienced person who, at the time of signing, is thinking only of going into business, not of getting out.[10]

Offering family-style dining at moderate prices, Long John Silver has nearly 500 restaurants across the country.

Summary and Conclusion

Every coin has two sides, and what may seem advantageous to one person in a franchise may be considered just the opposite by someone else. Much of the success of any franchise operation under a particular agreement is dependent upon the personality of the franchisee. Some people like a regimented system; others are more inclined to free-wheeling. Those interested in a franchise should seek not only the type of business in which they would be happiest, but also a franchisor with whom they would be compatible in terms of a working relationship.

From the standpoint of the prospective franchisee, a franchise will probably become a successful business sooner than a nonfranchised business. As the years go by, the franchise has the greater chance of surviving and prospering.

Franchises are clearly advantageous to the inexperienced person who is lacking in business skills. If the franchise is a retail business, completely designed layout, facilities, displays, and fixtures, as well as a proven management system are supplied. The franchisee's finances and credit standing are strengthened, and she or he can with limited capital, enter a business with a very favorable income potential. On the other hand, the prospective franchisee must determine if the costs of the franchise business are justified and decide if the constraints of the franchise agreement are tolerable.

For the franchisors, too, there are both advantages and disadvantages. Clearly, franchising offers a dynamic and powerful way to build an effective distribution network without a great deal of capital. And franchisees tend to be more highly motivated than salaried employees. But they can also display an independence which no employee would dare to. Finally, the franchisee can have all the requirements to make it but if he or she lacks one named guts, forget it.

The Franchise Agreement

Before entering into a franchise agreement, consider the story of the chicken and the pig. The chicken said to his friend the pig, Why don't we go into business together. I see a lot of ham and egg restaurants and I think you and I would make a fortune if we were to go into that type of business. The pig thought for a while and finally said no. The chicken, a little taken back, said, I don't understand why not. The pig said, You see, for you it's only an investment, for me it's a total commitment. Unless both parties are totally committed, franchisor and franchisee, it usually ends in divorce.

The franchise agreement is a contract. It meets the conditions of legality of purpose, offer and acceptance, consideration and, presumably, competent parties. Signed by both parties, it is enforceable in a court

The franchise agreement is a contract and, like a marriage, entails a continuing relationship with dependency on both sides.

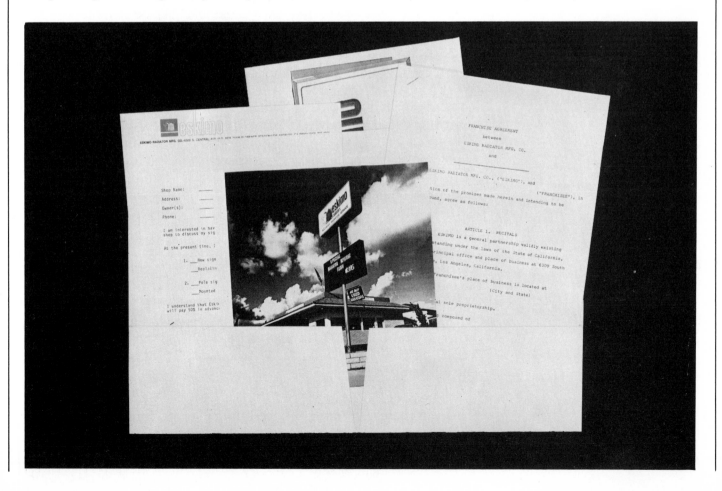

of law. Before signing a contract, the franchisee should understand that a binding commitment is being made, and that one cannot walk away from such a commitment without facing possible legal action. The same can be said to the franchisor.

In product franchises, the franchisees—or dealers—operate under a name of their own choosing. In the entire business format type of franchise—particularly one involving an established, well-known franchisor—the most valuable offer the franchisor makes is the right to use its name. Other promises are to provide varying forms of assistance to the franchisee.

In accepting the offer, the franchisee usually agrees to some monetary commitment in addition to operation of the franchise in a specified manner.

Both sides make commitments.

A Continuing Relationship

The contract will specify the duration of the franchise. In 1977—excluding contracts of automobile and truck dealers, gasoline service stations, and soft drink bottlers—over 80 percent of franchise agreements were for ten years or more; almost half were for twenty years or more.[1]

In reaching a franchise agreement, both parties agree to a continuing relationship. The franchisee and the franchisor are mutually dependent on each other—not just at the signing, but for the life of the contract. The importance of this relationship was stated by Monte E. Pendleton, president of Sun-X International Corporation, a franchisor:

Franchising is a method of distribution where there is a continuing relationship and dependency of the buyer and seller. It is best defined by the franchise agreements which each franchisor has with his particular franchisees. The most important factors in franchising are the continuing relationship and dependency.[2]

The length of the franchise is particularly important to the franchisee: It is a commitment, and one made for a protracted period of time. What happens if, after a few years, one finds that one doesn't like the business, or that there is too little free time, or that the business is not providing the income hoped for? While the franchisor will undoubtedly insist on the right of termination in the event the franchisee should not perform according to expectations, the franchisee should also seek the right to sell the business or to terminate the contract under reasonable circumstances.

General Franchisor Obligations

No franchisor's contract is identical to another's. In fact, there is often considerable variation in contracts between one particular franchisor and its franchisees. Some of these differences can be explained by different state laws, the stage of development of a franchise system when contracts are signed, or the territory involved—and there are other reasons. However, in addition to granting the rights to use its name, the franchisor will usually promise to provide at least some of the following:

1. Training

This can include training in the handling of the company's products and services—how to prepare food, for example, or the manner in which a service is provided. It might also include instruction in general business procedures, and specifically the methods to be followed to conform with the franchisor's systems in bookkeeping, purchasing, inventory control, personnel, and general policies.

2. Site Selection
This could involve not only selection of the site for the outlet, but also lease negotiations, arranging credit, construction, and maintenance. In some cases, the franchisor may already own the site.

3. Marketing and Advertising
A variety of activities might be included under such obligations: the development and placing of advertising; the running of promotions to increase store traffic; and the providing of point-of-sale material, banners, and other promotional items. In addition, the franchisor might promise to provide marketing information drawn from market surveys and to advise of successful promotions developed by other franchisees in different parts of the country.

4. Operating Systems
The franchisor might design and install systems for accounting and cost control, personnel management, inventory control, and other activities.

5. Continuing Managerial Assistance
This can be in the from of periodic visits by trained franchisor field personnel who can provide general management advice on how to adapt to local conditions. It could also entail periodic bulletins or newsletters to keep the franchisee abreast of developments within the franchise system and of competitive activities outside it.

6. Territorial Protection
If the franchisor grants an exclusive territory to a franchisee, it should protect this territory in accordance with contractual terms and any state or local laws that might apply.

7. Product Supply
The franchisor must provide a continuing supply of company products and supplies, as specified in the contract.

General Franchisee Obligations
In addition to an awareness of franchisor obligations, the franchisee must fully understand the extent of commitments made to the franchising company. Some of the obligations specify what the franchisee must do; others specify what not to do. The following are some of the obligations that might be called for:

1. Payment of Fees
Fees can take a variety of forms. There would probably be a one-time franchise fee, usually payable when the contract is signed. There may also be continuing fees due on a periodic basis. These are often based on a percentage of gross profits and cover advertising, rent, and other services. These are usually in addition to a royalty fee—also based on a percentage of gross profits and due on a periodic basis.

2. Business Hours
The franchisee may be required to be open during certain hours and days of the week, including holidays.

3. Business Methods
There may be a prescribed accounting method and the obligation to open the books to the franchisor for inspection during reasonable

business hours. Submission of periodic financial reports may be called for. There might even be the obligation to use a particular bookkeeping company.

4. Purchasing

The franchisee might be required to purchase all fixtures, equipment, or apparatus from the parent company or approved suppliers. This same mandate might apply to other suppliers of various types, or the franchisee might be prohibited from dealing with any supplier without prior franchisor approval.

5. Advertising and Promotion

In addition to paying a periodic advertising fee or a percentage of gross sales for advertising prepared and placed by the franchisor, the franchisee may be required to advertise locally, or to participate in sales drives, contests, or promotions developed by the parent company. There might also be a requirement to submit any locally prepared advertising for approval of the franchisor.

6. Employees

The parent company may insist on the right to approve of the franchisee's hired help. In some types of franchises, it is also fairly common for the franchisor to prescribe the uniforms to be worn.

7. Inventory

The franchisee might be required to maintain specific inventory levels of particular items.

8. Banking

A bank may be designated in which daily receipts must be deposited. The parent company might prohibit withdrawal of more than a certain percentage of net profits—or more than a certain weekly amount—for personal management.

9. Insurance

The types of coverage—and the amounts of coverage—are often mandated. In addition, the franchisee may be required to hold the parent company harmless from all claims arising out of the conduct of the franchised business.

10. Quality Standards

The franchisor may reserve the right to determine standards of quality, service, and production. This might also include the right to prohibit the franchisee from selling any products not made, designed, or approved by the parent company.

11. Pricing

Retail prices may be set by the franchisor.

12. Policy

The franchisee may be required to conduct the business in accordance with franchisor policies and regulations in existence at the signing of the contract, or as they may be issued from time to time after the signing of the contract. This condition might also include the prohibition of certain practices, such as selling on credit.

13. Disputes

It might be required that all disputes be submitted to compulsory arbitration.

14. Termination

The parent company may demand the right to purchase the franchisee's business at a specified price—or in accordance with a predetermined formula—if the franchise agreement is terminated for cause or at the will of the parent company. This is sometimes associated with the demand that the franchisee lease the outlet and the property on which it is located to the parent company and then take back a sublease which is cancellable for breach of contract.

15. Other Franchise Interests

The franchisee might be prohibited from conducting any other commercial business while still under contract to the franchisor.

These, in general, are the kinds of provisions that most franchise contracts are likely to contain. Only rarely will a contract contain all or even most of these conditions, but one can expect to find some of them in almost any franchise agreement.

Reasonableness of Contract Terms

There has been much criticism of the almost dictatorial terms imposed upon franchisees in franchise contracts. One writer, Harold Brown, believes that most franchise agreements are inherently unfair to the franchisee.[3]

The purpose of any contract is twofold. It documents the terms and agreements made between the parties to the contract and—ideally—serves as a protection for each party in all future disagreements.[4]

The critics, however, contend that lengthy and complicated contracts prepared by highly paid lawyers of large companies are often beyond the comprehension of the unsophisticated newcomer to the business world. Even when a franchisee's lawyer suggests modifications of the terms in the agreement, some franchisors will present the contract on a take-it-or-leave-it basis.[5]

Lack of precision in the wording of the contract is another criticism often leveled at franchisors—particularly as it affects the rights of the parent company. Most franchisors, it is claimed, will spell out precisely the franchisee's obligations while at the same time using language that allows for greater flexibility on the part of the franchise company.

While all of these criticisms are warranted, it is unfair to level them against all franchisors. The good and the bad exist in every segment of society and the business world, including franchising, but in deciding whether a particular franchisor's terms are either reasonable or unreasonable, one must also take into consideration what is at stake for the franchisor.

One of the many reasons for a franchise system's success is that it delivers a quality product or service at a sensible price. As pointed out earlier, franchising is not a business, but a method of distribution. Franchisees are not employees of the parent company, but independent business people. The whole is only as good as its parts.

The franchisor invests in advertising, training, and research and puts considerable time and effort into developing and distributing its product or service. The larger franchisors operate in a very competitive environment. It is understood that franchisee fees contribute to the costs of these activities. However, if a franchisee shows excessive independence, the quality of the product or service it delivers may suffer. If there are other outlets in the same area, they may all suffer because of one franchisee's delivery of subpar products or services. The franchisor certainly has the moral right—as well as the legal right—to see to it that its name and reputation, which have taken so long to develop, are upheld.

While no reasonable person will find fault with sensible provisions of a contract specifying standards of quality control, production, advertising, etc., some of the other conditions in the foregoing list might be questioned. Why, for example, might a contract specify a bank to be used by the franchisee? Suppose there are many franchised outlets in a particular area and that the bank also has many branches in the area. By channeling all deposits into that bank, the franchisor can possibly obtain more leverage with the bank. The company can then obtain credit more easily—not only for itself, but also for franchisees. And it might be able to do this at more favorable interest rates.

Or why specify a bookkeeping service? The situation may be similar to that of the bank. If it is a service with computerized data processing equipment, it has the capability of providing statistical data and financial reports on a large number of franchised outlets. It is a matter of convenience, efficiency, and lower cost.

There may also be perfectly valid reasons for differences in terms between a franchisor and its many franchisees. Part of the explanation may be found in the date the contracts were signed. A relatively new franchisor might be quite lenient in setting terms. A franchise in a well-established, successful system is certainly worth more than one in earlier stages of development, when the franchisor was just beginning expansion. A territory with great profit potential is also worth more than one in which the potential is limited, even if only in the short run.

Not all franchisors are paragons of virtue at all times, but if one will investigate why certain provisions are included in a contract—or why terms sometimes differ among franchisees—it will often be found that the reasons are perfectly valid.

Provisions of Primary Importance

It is obvious that many kinds of provisions may be found in a franchise contract. Each one is worthy of scrutiny. Are some more important than others? While there is some disagreement among students of franchising, Harry Kursh, author of *The Franchise Boom*, reports a general consensus, which tends to emphasize five areas of special importance: 1. territory and location; 2. franchise fees; 3. sales quotas; 4. the right to sell the franchise; 5. contract termination or cancellation.[6]

Territory and Location   Location refers to a specific place—the actual site or address of the outlet. A good location, especially for a retail outlet, might be one that is easy to get to and one with good exposure to potential customers. A location in a major shopping area, yet one also visible and easily accessible to passersby, might be considered ideal, but many other factors must be taken into consideration—lease rates, zoning laws, building costs and codes, the availability of utilities, real estate taxes, to name only a few. Many franchisors have real estate departments to handle such matters. Site location is best left to the experts.

Of equal—if not greater—importance to the franchisee is his territory. Territory refers to the geographic area in which a franchisee exclusively represents the franchisor. This territory might consist of a few blocks in a crowded city, town, or county, a large metropolitan area, or even a state or larger region. The size of the territory depends on—among other factors—the frequency of need or desire for the product or service marketed. It is quite reasonable to assume that a business service franchisee, for example, may require only one office in a fairly large area which could easily accommodate many fast-food establishments without one outlet encroaching on another's business.

The franchise companies tend to feel that they have the right to determine how many outlets can be placed in any given area. Franchisees, on the other hand, tend to want exclusivity in as large an area as possible. Surprisingly, though, territorial exclusivity may not always be to the franchisee's advantage. There is the case of Chicken Delight, a franchisor that was quite concerned about opening additional units in a given territory. However, it was discovered that when the company had five stores, sales of the original two rose. Apparently, the greater exposure attained by more outlets actually increased business for all of them.[7]

Franchise Fees The most common charge to a franchisee—particularly in entire business format type agreements—is the franchise fee. This is a fee of a fixed amount, generally due upon signing of the contract. Essentially, this is for the right to operate under the franchisor's name.

Almost as common is a royalty, payable at specified periods during the life of the contract. It is usually a percentage of gross sales and commonly ranges from about 2 to 5 percent.

Two other fees are quite common. One is a fee to cover the costs of advertising or marketing, whether the advertising is national or local. And if the franchisor owns—or holds the lease on—the site on which the outlet is located, there might be a rental fee. Both of these fees are also usually a percentage of gross sales.

Such fees represent a major cost to the franchisee, and they can vary widely among franchisors. Harry Kursh, who claims that there is little economic justification for such fees, makes a good point.[8] Consider, for example, a recent fee structure for two of the better-known fast-food restaurant franchises, McDonald's and Burger King (fees other than the initial franchise fee are percentages of gross sales).

Why is Burger King's franchise fee over three times larger than McDonald's? And why are their royalty and marketing fees a larger percentage of gross sales? Burger King might answer that they are a smaller franchise company and must charge more per outlet to provide comparable services and to be competitive in advertising.

In 1979, McDonald's gross sales approximated 5.4 billion dollars, while Burger King's were about 1.5 billion.[9] McDonald's had a little over twice as many franchisees as Burger King. Burger King's reasoning

Table 4-1

	McDonald's	Burger King
Franchise fee	$12,500	$40,000
Royalty	3%	3½%
Marketing fee (primarily advertising)	3%	4%
Rental fee	8½%	8½%

Source: Lee Smith, "Burger King Puts Down Its Dukes," *Fortune*, June 16, 1980.

It's not always so easy to have it your way at Burger King. Of the 10,000 franchise applications they receive each year, only a tenth are accepted.

might be justified, but—to the potential franchisee—is a Burger King worth that much more than a McDonald franchise? Burger King is apparently not concerned. They have recently been receiving about 10,000 franchise applications per year and accepting only a tenth of them. The average outlay in 1979—$179,000 per outlet, including equipment costs.[10]

One might also ask if the royalty and marketing fees are adjustable during the life of the contract. As the system grows in terms of total number of outlets, the cost of service and advertising per outlet should lessen. And the franchisee's outlet should be producing greater sales volume in future years. Under such circumstances, is it fair to charge the same percentage during the life of the contract? These are all questions which the prospective franchisee should ask.

There may also be other fees and charges, some a percentage of gross sales and others a fixed cost. These can include service fees, equipment rental, or penalties for nonobservance of contract terms. There may also be a termination penalty and a renewal fee. It is vital to fully understand the extent of the monetary commitment to be made—not just initially, but during the life of the contract.

It should be pointed out that many franchises cost much less than one for a McDonald's or a Burger King. Regardless of the franchisor, one should always attempt to negotiate the terms. If the franchisor's monetary terms are not negotiable, the prospective franchisee need not sign the contract but can always look elsewhere.

Sales Quotas Most franchisors want a sales quota provision in their contracts. It is their assurance that a franchisee who has been granted a territory will strive to reach at least a minimum sales level. Although it has been asserted that many franchisors do not really place much importance on quotas, it is also true that the franchisor could be in the position to terminate if the quota is not met. Therefore, it is extremely important that the prospective franchisee determine the "realism" of the quota before signing the contract.[11]

The Right to Sell the Franchise   As an independent business person owning a business, a franchisee naturally feels that she or he has the right to sell that business or to pledge it as collateral against a loan.

The franchisor, on the other hand, is likely to point out that a franchise is not like any other type of business. The franchisor has helped to set up the business. Not only does the franchisee operate under the parent company's name, but there is the advantage of continuing guidance and counsel and all the other benefits accruing as part of the franchise system. With this reasoning, a franchisor may feel quite justified in limiting the rights to sell the franchise.

The imprecision of language in some contracts (which has been the subject of criticism) is sometimes evident in clauses regarding the franchisee's right to sell. In others, however, it is quite precise.

As an example, one franchisor contract requires that any new party to whom the contract is assigned must be "a person who substantially meets company qualifications as to Franchise Owners and who undergoes the company's training program."[12]

In general, most franchisors will permit sale of the franchise, but they prefer that, in addition to meeting parent company qualifications, the new owner sign a new contract. Even if the new owner will not sign a contract, the franchisor will probably not oppose the sale, but then has the right to deny the new owner the use of the parent company's name, logo, trademarks, or patents. In addition, the franchisor could then open a new outlet across the street.

If a franchise contract absolutely denies the right to sell the franchise, then the franchisee is not really an independent business owner, but an affiliate of a chain. It is important that this and other rights be carefully spelled out in the contract. At the same time, it should be realized that a franchisor is not being unreasonable if it seeks to protect its patents and trademarks. Fairness to both sides should be the criterion.

Cancellation or Termination   Most franchise contracts will describe exactly why the agreement may be terminated. Failure to make payment of fees, violation of quality standards, failure to meet quotas, bankruptcy, even conviction for a felony are just some of the many conditions under which a franchisor may reserve the right to terminate the contract. It is important that the franchisee understand such clauses before signing the contract.

A critic of franchise contracts points out that often the causes for revocation are dispersed throughout the contract instead of being grouped under a specific, clear-cut heading titled "termination."[13] Just one more reason why the franchisee should be represented by a lawyer.

The franchisee may also be able to terminate a contract. This is frequently done for personal reasons. The franchisee may just not be suited to the role of small businessman or possibly the franchise has not produced enough income, despite the best efforts over a reasonable length of time.

Most termination clauses provide for advance notification. Often the stipulation is that such notices be submitted in writing at least ninety days before the termination is to take effect—regardless of which party is seeking to cancel.

Termination clauses should also specify the obligations of each party when a contract is terminated. The payment of debts, transfer of

The Franchise Agreement

property, and closing out of bank accounts are just some of the matters to be cleared up. Most importantly, are there any termination fees, and how much are they?

However, termination procedures are much less of a problem today than they were back in the 1950s and 1960s, when franchising was in the early stages of the tremendous growth it has experienced since the end of World War II. While franchisees should certainly insist that such rights be clearly phrased in the franchise agreement, the greater concern today is that of renewal rights upon expiration of the contract. The more reputable franchisors offer a renewal option on a first-refusal basis, although often for a shorter period of time than in the initial agreement. The inclusion of renewal rights—accurately and clearly stated—should be demanded by the prospective franchisee.

Negotiating the Franchise Agreement

To the layman, a contract can be a very forbidding document, often including legal terms or language that only a lawyer can understand and interpret. Time and again it has been strongly suggested in these pages that the potential franchisee obtain the services of a lawyer before signing a franchise contract.

It has been pointed out that there are few lawyers thoroughly versed in franchising. Although franchising is itself not a business, it is involved in distributing the products and services of many different businesses. Many state and federal laws apply specifically to these individual businesses, whether they are part of a franchise system or not. Again, franchising is a relatively new area; laws and regulations covering it have only recently been promulgated, and the field is still under study. Add to this the variety of contracts that often exist between one franchisor and its franchisees, and it is little wonder that there are few lawyers fully experienced in all aspects of franchising. However, a good lawyer can advise the potential franchisee of the full extent of the obligations called for, and whether or not they are reasonable. In fact, some of the more reputable franchisors will not permit a franchisee to sign a contract without legal representation.

Most writers and students of franchising have written little about negotiating a franchise agreement. To most franchisors, certain provisions of their contracts are sacrosanct—that is, unalterable. Other areas, however, may be negotiable. A person who has experience in running a business may seem a much more likely prospect to a franchisor than one who has not, and some terms of the contract might be adjusted accordingly. Or someone who already owns or has a lease on a piece of property ideally suited to a franchised outlet should be able to negotiate many of the terms.

It is best that a prospective franchisee learn as much as possible about franchising—and the type of business being considered—before beginning serious discussions with a franchisor. While the list of books on the subject is not extensive, a number of them are excellent. A good librarian can help in finding them; so can a bookstore that specializes in business books. There is also a bibliography at the end of this book. The Small Business Administration is a good source of information. Franchising has also been the subject of numerous newspaper and magazine articles. An accountant can prove helpful, too. Such a person can determine whether financing arrangements, interest rates, and bookkeeping requirements are both realistic and reasonable. There is also a growing body of franchise consultants (more will be said about them in a later chapter).

Finally, there is that good old attribute of plain common sense. Attorney Gerrold G. Van Cise has stated:

The franchise contract should be frank, fair and enforceable. The draftsman of this document should not be so open-minded in protecting the franchisee, however, that his brains fall out in failing to safeguard the franchisor. Thus, he should not fear to empower the franchisor to "coerce" and "dominate" the franchisee if any such restraint is reasonably necessary to prevent the latter from using the licensed name to destroy the franchisor or to defraud the public. But any excessive controls, which are not thus reasonably ancillary to the lawful main purpose of franchising, should be avoided. Our three guiding principles might be supplemented with a fourth: "Too much of anything is bad except whiskey."[14]

Summary and Conclusions

A franchise agreement calls for a commitment from both the franchisee and the franchisor. Both parties have obligations—not just at the signing of the contract, but during its life, or until termination.

The contract is a document which serves as the framework for operation of the franchise and for the relationship between franchisee

An Arthur Treacher's Fish & Chips restaurant. The advent of the two-paycheck family has made dining out a popular form of togetherness.

and franchisor. All the fees, terms, promises, and "ifs, ands, or buts" should be included in precise, understandable language.

To the individual interested in franchising, this chapter may sound foreboding. Its purpose is not to scare readers, but simply to alert them to the importance of the contract.

Most students of franchising feel that the contract is the most important factor in determining whether a franchise will be successful or not. Author Robert M. Dias wrote:

> *The franchise contract is the key to franchising success. In it are the ingredients of experience that insure success. The contract can, also, contain the seeds for disappointment and discontent which can spell failure for the investor, as well as the parent company.*[15]

A franchise agreement is not one to be entered into hastily. On the contrary, it should be approached with caution.

The best advice: Get a good franchise lawyer, accountant, and franchise consultant.

Hint: Ask for the names of clients they have represented. The best background is if they have advised both franchisor and franchisee and have—or had—clients in the type of business you are interested in. Remember—it's your money, so check their track record and their references before retaining them. Consider their cost to you as part of your franchise investment. Their advice could mean the difference between success and failure.

Finding and Evaluating Franchising Opportunities

5

Study Franchising First

Before plunging into any enterprise, it is just plain common sense to know as much about it as possible. You shop for a car by comparing prices; perhaps you read about the various models in a consumer-oriented magazine first. You might talk to others who already own a model you're interested in and, of course, you'll make test drives. A car is a big investment, and—before committing your money—you want to know what you're getting.

Becoming a franchisee entails more than a legal commitment and, unlike a car, it's more than a financial investment. It's a commitment of both your money and your time. When you sign a franchise agreement, you're signing up for the future. Such a step is not to be taken lightly.

The government has issued pamphlets, reports, and booklets on franchising. The Department of Commerce and the Small Business

Before committing money, be sure you know what you're getting.

Finding and Evaluating Franchising Opportunities

Administration have much printed information available. Trade organizations are another good source. Much of this material is also listed in the bibliography.

In addition to the available written material, there are other ways to learn about franchising. Here are some of them:

Educational Courses Many colleges offer business courses in the evening. Some are for credit; others are of the noncredit, adult-education variety. Check to see if any courses are given in small business management, including franchising. There are also seminars on franchising. New York University, for one, holds monthly seminars throughout the United States.

Trade Shows These will be advertised locally if they are to take place in your area. Look for titles such as "Start Your Own Business" or "Business Opportunities." Usually these trade shows are good for looking and learning—not for buying.

Answer Advertisements The material sent to you will reveal the promotional techniques of various franchisors and the variety of terms available, but prepare yourself for follow-up mail or phone calls.

Talk to Others If you know any people connected with franchising—perhaps a franchisor or franchisee—they can be helpful. Try to get both viewpoints. If you have answered advertisements, you might have the chance to talk with a franchise salesman sooner than anticipated. Listen, but don't sign—yet.

Write for Information There is an organization, called "The National Association of Franchised Businessmen," devoted to the needs and interests of franchisees. It can provide specific information.

These are the major ways in which you can investigate franchising. More detailed information is included in Chapter 8, "Where to Learn More about Franchising."

Understand the Franchisor's Needs

One of the advantages of franchising to the franchisor is that franchisees tend to be highly motivated. They're not employees working for a salary; they're independent business people who expect their incomes to be related to their efforts. They're the kind of people inclined to say: "The more I produce, the more I'll make."

However, as franchising has grown, and more and more of these highly motivated people have gone into business, they're becoming harder and harder to find. And most franchisors today require more than just high motivation—they also need people with money to invest. Even among those with the credit and ability to raise funds, not too many are willing to remortgage their house to go into business. The better franchisors also look for people with at least some managerial talent. In addition, they want prospects with the right psychological traits: self-assurance, the willingness to work hard, and a "take a chance" attitude, even though franchising offers a far better than average opportunity for success. The number of persons with all these characteristics has just not kept pace with the number of franchise offerings. In fact, some franchisors report that a shortage of qualified franchisees acts as an impediment to their future growth.[1]

Knowing this is helpful because the person interested in franchising can find clues as to where to look for the opportunities in U.S. Department of Commerce reports and elsewhere.

When to Join

At what stage of development would you like to join a franchise system? If you find a franchise which you think has great potential but is just coming into existence, you will probably find the terms very reasonable. The fees may be relatively small, the rights for a long time, the territory sizeable, and more than the usual number of terms may be negotiable. You may get the right to subfranchise. The short-run potential *might* not seem to be as good as in an already well established system with a readily recognizable name, but—if you can stick it out—the longer-run income potential can be extremely good because of the more favorable contract terms. The "might" is emphasized because it is possible that a new business offering a product or service that your market wants can, if properly promoted, do extremely well quite quickly.

The stage of development of a franchise system will have a bearing on its recruiting efforts. It can affect the number and type of people to be reached, and the manner in which the franchisor attempts to reach them.

The early stage of development could be called the initiation stage.[2] Start-up costs for developing a new system are generally quite high, and the franchisor will usually try to cover these costs by recruiting a fairly large number of franchisees as quickly as possible. Unless the product or service to be distributed calls for special talents, the franchisor probably will not be overly selective in the choice of franchisees at this stage of development.

Advertising copy in recruiting advertisements, and the medium in which the advertising appears, can be studied, although the need to recruit quickly may dictate general publications with large circulations. At this stage, the franchisor will also be evaluating the types of people that are attracted by the advertising.

The second stage of a franchise system's development could be called the growth or expansion phase.[3] The franchisor has completed the initial stage and has the first string of outlets in place. The franchisor has learned more about franchisees and can better pinpoint the qualifications for new ones. The advertising has been tested and the field staff has gained valuable experience.

The franchisor can now refine recruiting techniques. Some referrals may come from other franchisees. Word-of-mouth advertising can provide more prospects. Advertising copy can be fine-tuned, and advertising media can be more wisely selected. General publications with large circulations will probably continue to be used, but more selective media can be added to the schedule. Radio and television may also be used.

If the franchisor considered initial efforts to be successful, perhaps now the contract should be revised. The fees might be higher, other terms changed, and the number of negotiable terms reduced.

The franchise system should now be easier to evaluate than before. There are more outlets to visit, more franchisees to talk to. The fees and other terms might still be considered reasonable; it might still be a good ground-floor opportunity.

Finally, however, a franchise system will reach what can be called its maturity stage.[4] At this point in time, outlets are established in the desired markets. There could even be a situation in which the parent company is more interested in operating company-owned outlets. Recruitment advertising will now concentrate on specific markets,

Finding and Evaluating Franchising Opportunities

or—through the use of selective media—on people with specific characteristics. A franchisor with a good reputation may actually have a waiting list of applicants, and recruitment advertising may cease entirely. Word-of-mouth and personal referrals will bring in more applicants than before. Franchisors point out that personal referrals can be converted at a 50-percent success rate, compared to about a 5-percent rate for leads acquired through advertising.[5]

Franchisors can now pick and choose new franchisees. It will be considerably more difficult for the interested investor to get a franchise, and the terms will be much more difficult to negotiate. However, the risks may now be less and, with a good product or service under a respected banner, the profit potential promising.

Recruitment Media Used by Franchisors

There are many different media which franchisors can use to attract potential franchisees, and few franchisors are known to rely on a single method of advertising.[6] It can vary—as you have seen—according to the stage of development of the franchise system. It can be media with widespread appeal, or media which is specifically directed at a target audience in terms of age, income, sex, education, occupation, or interests.

Here are the pros and cons—from the franchisor's viewpoint—of some of them.

National Newspapers There are very few national newspapers, and the most prominent is the *Wall Street Journal*. It reaches a relatively high-income audience of business people. Part of the classified section is devoted to "Business Opportunities"—and this is the usual place to look for franchise opportunities. For no particular reason, most of this advertising seems to appear on Thursdays. The *Wall Street Journal* is also used when franchisors want to impress the financial community.

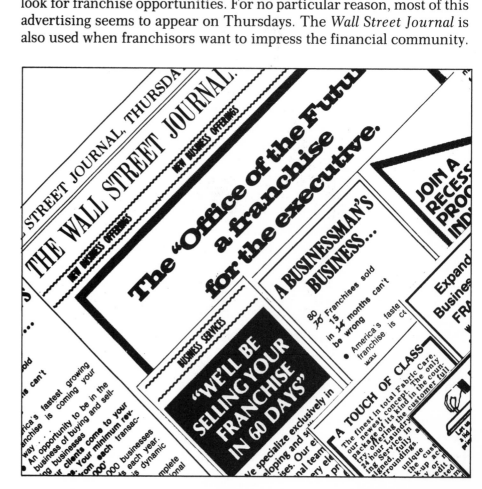

A surprisingly large percentage of the circulation of the *New York Times* is delivered outside the metropolitan New York area, particularly on Sunday, when its circulation is much larger than on weekdays. It, too, reaches a relatively high-income audience. Look in the classified portion of the business section.

According to the Conference Board, about 45 percent of the franchisors that it surveyed favor national newspapers for recruiting purposes.[7]

Local Newspapers A franchisor who is expanding on a regional basis will use local papers to zero in on particular markets. These can include big city papers whose larger Sunday circulations reach out into a larger geographic area than on weekdays. They can be used in both the initiation and the growth stages. In the maturity stage, they might be used when the franchisor is seeking recruits in particular markets only. Again, look under "Business Opportunities" in either the classified or business sections.

National Consumer Magazines National magazines such as *Time* and *Newsweek* are usually considered far too expensive for recruitment advertising. Occasionally, a major national franchisor will schedule consumer advertising in them with a small portion directed toward interested prospects, but this is unusual. But consumer advertising can, of course, influence those considering franchising as a business.

Radio and Television These media are also extremely expensive and are rarely used for recruiting. As with national consumer magazines, there is just too much waste—that is, the advertiser is paying too much to reach too many viewers or listeners who are not likely prospects. Most big franchisors use them for product or service advertising which is directed at the user. Such advertising can, however, make recruitment advertising in other media more effective.

Finding and Evaluating Franchising Opportunities

Direct Mail This is a method which permits franchisors to concentrate on what are considered highly likely prospects. Mailing lists can be purchased from firms which specialize in compiling them. These lists can be targeted at audiences with very specific characteristics on a local, regional, or national scale. A single mailing or a series of them can be made. It is the "rifle-instead-of-the-shotgun" approach.

Franchise Exhibits More and more go-into-business-for-yourself-type trade shows are being scheduled. They can last from a day or two to a week and are held at various times in community centers, convention halls, and other large exhibit centers. Franchisors—particularly the new and smaller ones—will participate by renting exhibit space. Such shows are usually advertised on local radio and television, or in the local newspaper.

Permanent Franchise Showrooms These are a fairly recent innovation and are usually set up by promoters who serve as sales agents for several different franchisors. There are a number of such permanent showrooms across the country. They are usually used by relatively new franchisors in their formative stages.[8]

Looking for Specific Franchise Opportunities

You can learn about franchise opportunities by reading the recruitment advertising in the media just outlined or by attending shows and exhibits, but you won't learn about all of them, and therefore you should also investigate other sources. Some of these other sources are

Franchise Directories There are several excellent directories of franchise opportunities which are readily available. Among these is the extensive *The Franchise Opportunities Handbook* published by the U.S. Department of Commerce and the Office of Minority Business Enterprise. In addition to providing information on various franchise opportunities, this directory—which is published annually—provides information on government assistance programs, nongovernment assistance programs, and other sources of information. More information on this and other directories can be found in Chapter 8.

Specialty Publications There are many specialty publications that can be useful to those interested in franchising. Some of these could have been listed under recruitment media, but they are listed here because the editorial content could be of particular interest. Magazines such as *Entrepreneur* and *Venture* are written for the small businessman and often include articles on franchising.

If you have a specific business in mind, there is undoubtedly a trade publication devoted exclusively to that business. If you visit franchisees during your investigations, ask the proprietor which trade magazine he reads and ask to look at a copy. If it looks interesting, jot down the name and address of the publisher and send away for a subscription. If there are franchise recruitment advertisements in this publication, most of them would apply to the specific business covered editorially.

Franchise Marketing Agencies and Consultants While relatively new to the industry, both marketing agencies and consultants show prospects of becoming very important parts of the growth of franchising. Consultants serve in a variety of ways, from helping the prospective franchisee decide what type of business would best suit him to evaluating the worth of specific franchise offerings.

After your friends tell you what you want to hear and before the dream comes true, there are other references you may wish to consult.

Other Sources Talking to other franchisees has already been mentioned, but there are other people who can also help. Friends may know little about franchising, but they may know someone else who does. You can talk to bankers, brokers, or equipment suppliers. Or, if a particular franchise system appeals to you, write directly to the parent company. If you attend a seminar or take a course in franchising, you should look for leads there, too.

Chapter 8, "Where to Learn More about Franchising," will provide more detailed information on sources, including addresses.

Evaluating Franchise Opportunities

If you thoroughly study the franchise recruitment advertising and can attend a trade show or an exhibit, you may well be flabbergasted by the great variety of franchises available, and by the multitude of products and services marketed by franchisors. If you answer some of the advertisements, you'll be amazed by the variety of fees, terms, and initial investments required. There will, however, be one similarity in all the literature you will receive—and that is the promise of financial success.

With all these "sure-thing" opportunities, how do you decide in which one you'll invest your money? Are they all as good as they sound? Unlikely, but how do you separate the good from the bad?

Some of the investigative procedures have already been mentioned, but they bear repeating. Others have not, and they should all be followed before you put your signature to that contract.

Investigate the franchise company first. Find out how long it has been in business. If it has been in existence for a number of years, there must be a good reason for it. This is not to say that a relatively new company is not a good investment—far from it—but a company that has been in business for a while has a history that you can study, a track record that you can look into. Dun & Bradstreet can provide a

Finding and Evaluating Franchising Opportunities

credit rating. The Chamber of Commerce or the Better Business Bureau may be able to provide vital information. How well regarded is the franchisor by the National Association of Franchised Businessmen? Write to them and find out. What are the bank references? From such sources, you can get an idea of the soundness of the company's financial position and of its business practices.

If you haven't yet visited franchisees, you should do so if the franchise company has passed this first phase of your investigation. If it's not one of those big companies with many outlets, get a list of franchisees in the geographic area you're considering. If it's a retail franchise, visit the outlet during business hours and begin by just observing. What is the traffic pattern of customers? What are they buying? Is the interior decor clean and attractive? Is it appealing from the outside? Is there enough parking space? Is the help well trained and courteous? After this visual inspection, try to talk with the franchisee. Ask about profitability and the support and back-up provided by the franchisor. Reread Chapter 3, "The Advantages and Disadvantages of Franchising," and systematically discuss the points listed. Inquire, too, about the contract. In the opinion of the franchisee, were the negotiations fair, and are the terms reasonable?

If the franchisor passes these two tests, consider now the product or service marketed. Does the product fit the geographic area you're considering. You're not going to sell a lot of snowshoes in Florida. Is it a seasonal product and, if so, will the franchise provide enough income to carry you through the off-season? Is it a staple or a luxury? What is the potential for repeat business? How does the product look to you personally? Is it priced competitively? Is it of good quality? Would you buy it?

What about territory and location? Location, as you should remember, is the actual site or address of the outlet. Territory is that area in which you would exclusively represent the franchisor. Is that territory guaranteed in the contract, and will the franchisor protect it? Check with other franchisees and with legal counsel. Will the guarantee stand up in court? Is the territory big enough, with the potential to provide sales that will cover costs and produce sufficient profits which, after deducting fees and charges, will yield a good income?

So far, it seems, everything looks good. You decide to proceed to the contract stage. You now take all the precautions you should. You are represented by a good lawyer, and your accountant has advised that the financial terms are fair and reasonable, but—no matter how carefully the terms have been negotiated and how precise the language—there may still be room for interpretation. Earlier talks with franchisees have given you an idea of the relationship between the parent company and its franchisees, but reconfirm what you've learned. Ask specific questions about training, business forms, advertising, continuing assistance, and so forth. Does it seem that you will be treated like an employee instead of a business associate? Be sure you know before you sign the contract.

Danger Signs

How can you tell the trustworthy franchisor from the hustler? Distinguish a sound investment from "pie-in-the-sky"?

Sadly, there is no sure-fire way. Franchising has grown so rapidly that it was inevitable that shady or downright fraudulent operators would move in to make a fast buck. They can all quote P. T. Barnum's famous line, "There's a sucker born every minute." Those who have been bilked could testify to the persuasiveness of unethical franchisors. The need for state laws and the issuance of regulations by the FTC is another indication that not everything in the field of franchising has been above-board.

How can you prevent becoming another one of those suckers? Investigating a franchise thoroughly is still the best way. However, this is another area which calls for good old common sense.

Put yourself in the shoes of a franchisor that wants to expand a business honestly and stay in business over the long run. He can't succeed unless the franchisees succeed. He can't afford to select unqualified applicants, and all applicants will be carefully screened. If a franchisor wants you to sign up at the first meeting, beware. If there's a high initial fee and little or no royalty based on future gross sales, take care.

One of the typical schemes used by fraudulent operators is the get-rich-quick promise with a big exclusive territory for your money. If a product is involved, you'll be required to stock up and, of course, pay for the inventory immediately. If the goods ever arrive, they'll be of poor quality and overpriced—goods that nobody will ever buy.

Watch out, too, for the pyramid distributor. The approach is similar to the one above—a get-rich-quick promise with an exclusive distributorship. The emphasis, though, will be on recruiting subdistributors. It's like a chain letter and, when the franchisee discovers the dishonesty, he's stuck. He becomes an accomplice because the only way he can recover his investment is to sell the distributorship. When the emphasis is on signing up others instead of selling a product or service, there's every reason for suspicion.

There are only three rules to observe in choosing your franchise site: location, location, and location.

Then there's the would-be franchisor who really isn't. If you answer one of their advertisements—which promise big profits with a small investment—you could meet a high-pressure salesman selling equipment such as vending machines. All you have to do is buy the machines, and the world is yours. Unfortunately, you'll probably end up with very expensive equipment that doesn't work.

Another ruse is the selective approach—often used with gullible prospects such as independent tradesmen or contractors in small towns. The ploy is that the person approached is the best man for the job because of his experience. It's all very flattering. The franchise entails the purchase of special kits for, say, swimming pools, but if the franchisee finds no market for swimming pools, he's still obligated to pay for the kits.

The list of fraudulent schemes can go on and on. To avoid being taken in, the cardinal rule is still "investigate before investing." Investigating takes time, however, and your time is not well spent investigating those operating on the border between honesty and deceit, or those that are absolute frauds. If you can spot the likely frauds first, your time can be devoted to studying the better prospects. Again, there's no sure-fire way to spot frauds, but the checklist that follows will help. Watch out for:

1. Exaggerated advertising appeals, especially the deal that promises spectacular profits for a low investment.

2. The fast-talking high-pressure salesman who insists on a fast signing of the contract.

3. The "overly reasonable" representative who, with calculated sincerity, appears willing to make every possible concession to you in a contract.

4. The "franchisor" who tried to convince you of his integrity because a reputable publication has been running his advertisements.

5. Contracts weighed too heavily in favor of the franchisor, especially those agreements that do not leave the franchisee with power to make decisions.

6. Unjustified franchise fees.

7. Grossly exaggerated potential earning.

8. Royalty payments or other financing charges that are out of proportion with sales volume and projected profits.

9. Overpricing of initial equipment.

10. Franchisors whose real business is selling franchises only.

11. Parent companies with a record of business failures.[9]

Hint: Be especially careful of anyone asking for a percentage of your *gross* profits. For instance, 5 percent of your gross sales could make the franchisor a half-partner who gets 100 percent of the *net* pretax profit. If you gross $200,000, for example, 5 percent of the $200,000 gross sales equals $10,000. If you net $10,000 before taxes, the franchisor's 5 percent of gross equals 100 percent of your net. Check these figures in Table 5–1. On sales of $200,000, franchisor's share is $10,000; Village Hardware now has zero profit instead of a $10,000 net profit (before taxes).

Table 5-1

Village Hardware Income Statement
1980

	$	% Sales
Sales	$200,000	100.0%
Cost of goods sold	130,000	65.0%
Gross profit	$ 70,000	35.0%
Operating expenses		
Owner's salary	$12,000	6.0%
Sales personnel salaries	16,000	8.0
Clerical salary	8,000	4.0
Payroll taxes	2,000	1.0
Employee benefits	1,000	0.5
Rent	5,000	2.5
Utilities	2,000	1.0
Advertising	2,000	1.0
Delivery	1,000	0.5
Travel	2,000	1.0
Telephone	1,000	0.5
Bad Debts	2,000	1.0
Supplies	2,000	1.0
Insurance	2,000	1.0
Depreciation	1,000	0.5
Interest	1,000	0.5
Miscellaneous	—	0.0
Total operating expenses	$ 60,000	30.0%
Net profit (before income tax)	$ 10,000 or	5.0%

Opportunities for Minority Franchisees Continue to Grow

Minority participation in business format franchising continues to expand, minority-owned franchised outlets increasing by over 23 percent in 1978. Of the 1,394 franchisors surveyed, 441 companies reported a total of 5,859 units owned by minority group business persons, while 907 reported no minority-owned units; the remaining companies—mostly large franchisors with a total of 45,995 franchisee-owned units—were not able to respond since they do not maintain and are not required to maintain records identifying minorities.

Data were not collected for automobile and truck dealers, gasoline service stations, and soft drink bottlers, but the Minority Business Development Agency of the U.S. Department of Commerce has estimated that in 1978 there were 12,211 minority-owned gasoline service stations and 321 automobile and truck dealers. The number of minority-owned gasoline service stations declined slightly from the 12,520 reported in 1977, due to the closing of over 4,000 gasoline stations, while automobile and truck dealers rose from 302.

Of the 5,859 minority-owned outlets, 2,584 were owned by blacks, 2,031 by persons with Spanish surnames, 1,100 by Orientals, and 144 by American Indians. Many minority-owned businesses are concentrated in the most popular franchising sectors, e.g., 1,582 in automo-

The Small Business Administration has provided low-interest loans to many minority persons to open their own businesses. Automotive products and services and fast-food restaurants account for almost half the minority-owned franchises in the United States.

tive products and services, 1,108 in fast-food restaurants, 655 in food retailing other than convenience stores, 613 in nonfood retailing, and 591 in convenience stores.

Small investors, especially minority entrepreneurs, often face two major obstacles in their efforts to operate a successful company: inexperience in business and management, and inadequate financing. The franchising system provides a means for lowering such barriers to entry. Under the franchise system, a franchisor usually provides managerial training and assistance on a continuing basis, and in many cases, finances the purchase of necessary equipment. The franchisor may also arrange for property leases, help obtain loans from the Small Business Administration, local banks, or other private investors, and, in some instances, may participate in the venture. In addition, franchisors generally provide such services as location analysis, advertising and merchandising, counseling and assistance, standardized procedures and operations, and sometimes centralized purchasing.[10]

Summary and Conclusions

Like a baseball player on a hitting streak, franchising is hot. From 1979 to 1980, according to *The Franchise Annual*, the number of franchisors in the United States jumped from 1,311 to 1,711. The publisher's president, Edward L. Dixon, says that this is the biggest jump in the ten-year history of the annual. "For years, we've been going up a couple of hundred annually. Now, we'll easily jump at least another 300 by 1981," he predicts.

Under these circumstances, finding the franchise opportunities should not be difficult. Evaluating them will—simply because of the ever-increasing number of franchisors, the number of products and services to be marketed, and the variety of terms and conditions offered. And, despite new laws and regulations, the chances of your meeting the "fast-buck" artist will be the same as ever, if not higher.

Despite the advice to learn all one can about franchising and to thoroughly investigate before investing, there will still be those poor souls who throw caution to the wind, sign a contract too hastily, and find themselves in a situation they didn't expect—and can't get out of.

Don't you be one of them. Take your time, seek good counsel and advice, and investigate thoroughly.

Then—and only then—should you make a commitment.

Franchise Financing

6

Today's Borrowing Climate

One of the great advantages of franchising to the franchisor is the ability to expand by using other people's money. The franchisor does incur legal costs involved in meeting federal and state requirements and in drawing up contracts, in addition to expenses for advertising, selling, training, and, perhaps, real estate operations. For example, a typical analysis of costs for a franchisor to set up one franchisee might be as follows:

Cost to Franchisee

Franchise fee	$15,000

Cost to Franchisor

Site selection	$ 3,000	
Recruitment advertising	1,500	
Franchise salesman	3,000	
Training	5,000	
Legal costs	1,000	
Total costs to franchisor	$13,500	$13,500
Balance retained by franchisor		$ 1,500

There are more than 350 franchisors in the fast-food field, which is one of the most competitive areas of franchising. This familiar sign is seen all over the country.

While the franchisor incurs costs, it is the franchisee who pays the franchise fee and, usually, the cost of equipment, opening inventory, and all the other costs involved in starting a business. As this book is being written, in the summer of 1980, the prime rate has just dropped below 11 percent. The prime rate applies to a bank's best blue-chip customers, such as big corporations, and the average individual will be required to pay at least two percentage points more. If a franchisee is to finance even part of the start-up costs, interest alone becomes a considerable expense. With the average start-up costs of $179,000 for a Burger King franchise,[1] interest costs alone could be at least $20,000 for the first year.

Many economists and students of franchising are predicting a trend to less capital-intensive franchises, where start-up costs to a franchisee will be much less than for, say, a fast-food restaurant. The service franchises, for example, cost far less to start.[2] Capital requirements to start a franchise in a business such as accounting, tax, and financial services, for example, range from $1,500 to about $50,000. These estimates are, admittedly, the minimum, but many franchises require far less than $100,000 to get started.

Most people, however, do not have $10,000 to $50,000 sitting in a savings account, and raising the required funds will take considerable time and effort and, probably, not only interest payments but the pledging of collateral. Many franchisors not only will advise a prospective franchisee on capital requirements but will also assist, in some way, in financing. Others will not. Part of your investigation of a franchisor should ascertain if financing assistance might be provided. If not, the franchisor might command such respect in the financial community that a bank loan will be relatively easy to obtain. In other cases, you'll be entirely on your own.

Selling Yourself

Regardless of where you obtain the needed funds, the first thing you must do is sell yourself. What's your business background? Are you credit-worthy? Are you the kind of person who is considered a good prospect, not only for running a business, but also for assuming a financial obligation?

Both the franchisor and the lending source will want to know about your business background. The best way to provide this is with a resume. There are two basic resume formats, the functional and the chronological. Whichever format you use, try to tailor it to the type of business your franchise would represent.

The chronological resume lists the various jobs you have held in chronological order, last job first, with a reasonably brief description of your responsibilities and accomplishments in each. The functional resume emphasizes the types of things you have done, for instance bookkeeping, statistical analysis, data processing, or financial reporting. Or it could be machine experience, carpentry, auto repair, or other related manual skills. A listing of where you worked, with the dates of employment, should follow. If experience you have gained in activities outside of your job applies to the franchisor's business, be sure to include it; also your education. If you have not written a resume before, you can probably find someone to help. Look under "resumes" in the Yellow Pages.

Next, check your credit rating. By law, credit bureaus must provide all information they have that relates to you. If there is any wrong

information in your file, have it corrected. If there is anything in your file that might be considered negative, be sure to have a good explanation for it.

Another step you should take is to prepare a financial balance sheet on yourself. A balance sheet is nothing more than the value of your assets less your financial obligations. The difference between the two is your net worth. It might be advisable to have an accountant help you with this. The size of your net worth might surprise you and provide insights as to where you might obtain funds at relatively low interest rates.

Start with the Franchisor

If you have selected a franchisor which your investigation reveals will provide some form of financial assistance, you are now ready to approach the parent company. You have learned all you can about franchising in general and can talk intelligently about it. You have studied the franchisor's business and your resume reflects the experience and ability to become a successful franchisee. Your credit rating is good, and your net worth indicates financial stability and the ability to raise capital. You also have a financial cushion to tide you over the early stages of the franchise, when sales may be low. The franchisor is impressed. He'll not only help you to finance your franchise, he'll do so to the maximum amount policy permits. Or he'll vouch for you with financial sources with whom he's done business before, sources that have, perhaps, financed other franchisees in the same system.

"Great," you say. But a word of caution. This is the time to reconfirm start-up costs. Make sure there are no hidden charges. Start-up costs will include at least the following, as reflected in a hypothetical new franchise:

	Capital Required	
	Total Investment	Cash Required
Franchise fee	$ 15,000	$ 15,000
Equipment package*	75,000	25,000
Supplies (basic inventory)	10,000	10,000
Security or leasehold	5,000	5,000
Working capital	10,000	10,000
Total	$115,000	$ 65,000

*Balance of $50,000 on equipment to be financed over a five-year period.

You should also attempt to estimate, with the franchisor's help, operating costs. While every business is different, certain costs are typical of almost every franchise operation. The table that follows lists both income and expenses for a food outlet grossing $500,000 a year. Note that the figures include not only the costs of goods sold (food and paper), but also operating expenses. These expenses should be estimated on a monthly basis for your specific business. When you think you have a good estimate of such expenses, check them with an accountant or, perhaps, another franchisee, to see if your estimates are reasonable.

Table 6-1

Projected Franchisee's Profit and Loss at the $500,000 Gross Sales Level

		Dollars	Percent of Total Sales
Gross sales		$500,000	100.0%
Cost of goods sold:			
Food	$219,000		43.8
Paper	10,000		2.0
Total Cost of Goods Sold	$229,000	$229,000	45.8
Gross margin		$271,000	54.2
Total expenses		$225,000	45.0
Net profit B/T		$ 46,000	9.2
Expenses			
Payroll and taxes		$100,000	20.0
Laundry and supplies		7,000	1.4
Utilities and telephone		15,000	3.0
Property taxes		3,000	.6
Insurance		2,000	.4
Maint. and repairs		4,000	.8
Advertising		15,000	3.0
Office expenses		1,000	.2
Royalties		20,000	4.0
Rent		40,000	8.0
Breakage		3,000	.6
Misc.		2,000	.4
Profession fees		1,000	.2
Interest expenses*		5,500	.11
Equip. depreciation**		7,500	1.5
Total expenses		$226,000	47.0%

* Interest rate on the $50,000 equipment package financing reflects 11% added onto going rate.
**Equipment depreciation is calculated on a straight line depreciation basis over a 10-year period.

Expenses don't always remain the same, however. As sales increase, so will some of the outlays, but they should not rise at the same rate as sales. In other words, as sales increase, expense factors should be more efficiently utilized. In addition to estimating your expenses at various sales levels, you should prepare a break-even chart which will give you an idea of how long it will take you to make a profit.

How to Figure the Break-Even Point of Your Business

You've been working hard serving your customers—so hard that you were sure you had a prosperous year. Yet at the end of the year, you've discovered that instead of a big juicy profit you've made a very small one (or perhaps have actually incurred a *LOSS!*).

What's the reason? Perhaps you have failed to keep tabs on the break-even point of your business.

What *is* the break-even point? How do you recognize it?

It's a place in your business operation where you neither make nor lose money. It means that you have covered your bare expenses only—from which point you need additional sales to bring you a profit.

To phrase it another way, you reach your break-even point when your gross profits equal the sum of your fixed and your controllable expenses.

To break this down to simple layman language, let's say you are a small businessman doing an average business of $3,900 a month.

To get your break-even point, write down the following:

1. Decide what your *fixed expenses* are. By fixed expenses we mean rent, insurance, various taxes you pay, utilities, depreciation—items that remain constant and do not change with the amount of business you do. Let's say that your fixed expenses amount to $600 a month.

2. Next, write down your maximum sales volume for a month (100 percent of potential volume). This would be $3,900.

3. Next, figure your *variable expenses* (expenses that ordinarily increase as your sales increase). These include outside labor, operating supplies, gross wages, repairs and maintenance, advertising, car and delivery, bad debts, administrative and legal expenses, and miscellaneous expenses. Let us assume that you have determined from your records that the average monthly sales can be expected to be about 80 percent of maximum potential ($3,100). You will then determine your variable expenses for a $3,100 volume. Let us assume that you arrive at $2,100 (about 80 percent of $3,100).

4. Write down the sum of your fixed expenses ($600) and your variable expenses ($2,100). This would give you a *total expense* of $2,700.

Equipped with these figures, you're now ready to prepare your BREAK-EVEN CHART. This "pictures" to you the point where your business has reached a break-even spot, under a given set of conditions.

How to Prepare Your Break-Even Chart

1. Draw a blank chart like the one shown. This will have equal horizontal divisions, which you will number 0, 10, 20, 30, and so on to 100, representing 0 percent to 100 percent.

2. Your vertical divisions will, in this example, run from $0 to $3,900. We decided to make each vertical division represent $100 in sales, so we numbered the lines 0, 3, 6, 9 and so on to 39. (Any equal division will do).

3. Add a diagonal line running from $0 to $3,900. This would be the line A–B shown. Label this *Sales.*

4. Rule a horizontal line at $600. This shows your fixed expenses, which stay about the same every month, regardless of sales. This is shown as line C–D on our chart. Label it *Fixed Expenses*.

5. In our example it was determined that average expected sales would be 80 percent of maximum potential, and that *total expenses* would be $2,700. Run a finger up the vertical line at 80, and another finger across the horizontal line at $2,700. Mark a dot or small x at the point where these two lines meet. This is shown as point E on our chart.

6. Draw a line from $600 at 0 percent to point E. This is shown as line C–E on our chart. Label this *Total Expenses*.

7. Where lines A–B and C–E cross each other is your *break-even point*. This is shown at point P.

8. Point P in our example falls at $1,800, which is approximately 45 percent of maximum sales potential. This means that you have to do business amounting to $1,800 to break even—that is, to cover your expenses. You are neither losing money nor making any profit at that point.

What Can a Break-Even Chart Tell You?

1. Our example tells you, for instance, that for the particular month in question, if you expect to make any profit, it must come from sales over and above $1,800.

2. It can tell you when your sales are not all they should be, and signals you to do something about your selling method, or your staff, or your merchandise lines.

3. It can help you control your budget by telling you what changes, if any, you might have to make to bring expenses in line with income.

4. It can tell you how much business you can afford to lose before you risk seeing your profits disappear—as well as how profits will increase with sales volume.

5. It can tell you what would happen if you were to increase or reduce prices.

6. It can tell you if you can afford to raise salaries—or whether a reduction in expenses is indicated.

7. It can help you appraise your merchandising policy. A break-even chart for each line could tell you which lines should be pushed, and which might be eliminated.

8. It can tell you in advance if you can afford to make improvements which might affect your expense structure.

Prepare a Break-Even Chart for Each Month.   Each month, know how much business you must do. Make up your chart *before* the start of the month. For long-range planning you can make up break-even charts for six-month periods or longer. In this way you will be charting your course to greater and more consistent profits—and know where you are going at all times.

Chart's Value Depends on Good Records.   A break-even chart, as a reliable warning system, is only as good as the accuracy of the figures from which it is built. It is of the utmost importance to have a good,

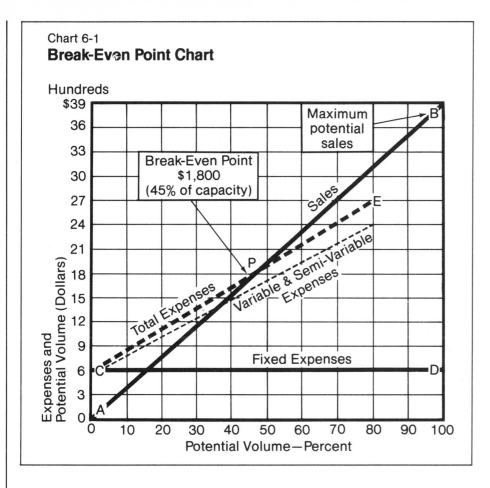

Chart 6-1
Break-Even Point Chart

Hundreds

Break-Even Point $1,800 (45% of capacity)

Maximum potential sales

Sales

Total Expenses

Variable & Semi-Variable Expenses

Fixed Expenses

Expenses and Potential Volume (Dollars)

Potential Volume—Percent

simple record-keeping system that accurately reflects sales and expenses day by day. Therefore, actually, step number 1 in constructing a break-even chart is: *have a good record-keeping system, and keep it in order!*

Banks

If the franchisor does not provide financial help, or will finance only part of your start-up costs, you must raise the balance. The most obvious place is your local bank. You should approach the bank with the same material with which you approached the franchisor. After talking with the franchisor, however, you now have the analysis of costs and an estimated break-even point. All of these documents should be neatly arranged and put in a folder.

Bankers are good businessmen. They have to be. Loan officers and loan committee members must be well read in business matters if they are to make intelligent loan decisions. They talk to other businessmen. They are aware of economic conditions and the forecasts and are intimately familiar with the area that they serve. They will want to know if you have a sound financial plan in mind, and if you know the business you're going into. The better the presentation you can make, the better your chances for loan approval. If the sum to be borrowed is sizeable, you might want to have an accountant assist you in preparing the presentation, and you might even want to talk with a franchise consultant.

The bank will also want to know what your living expenses are, for you're going to need sufficient funds to carry you through the early stages of your business. An amount equal to three times your monthly living expenses is the minimum that should be covered. Six months is preferable, and some banks, depending on the type of business you're entering, would prefer to see provision made for nine months or a year.

If a bank turns you down, try to find out why. If you are given a good reason, make the necessary adjustments in your presentation and try another bank.

There are many types of bank loans, and the one you're most likely to receive is dependent upon the size of the loan, its purpose, and the collateral, if any, that is required. Following are some of them:

Straight commercial loans: usually thirty to sixty days. These loans are based on submitting financial statements. This type of loan is generally secured for seasonal financing or inventory expansion.

Installment loan: usually longer-term loans repaid on a monthly basis. These repayment schedules can be tailored to the business needs, with heavier repayment during the peak business months and smaller payments during the slow season.

Term loans: usually have maturities of one to ten years and may be either secured or unsecured. Repayments can be either monthly, quarterly, semiannually, or annually. Early repayments are usually smaller, with a large final payment. Although many term loans are backed by collateral security, the bank ordinarily requires that current assets of the borrowing business exceed liabilities by the ratio of at least two to one (which means, in most cases, that this is not a loan for a start-up business).

Warehouse receipt loans: Under this form of financing, goods are stored in a warehouse and the warehouse receipt is given to the bank as security for a loan to pay off the supplier.

Equipment loan: These loans are made to finance the purchase of equipment. The lender usually retains title to the equipment until payments have been made. Such loans, when taken from a bank, are often obtained at lower interest rates than similar loans from other sources.

Collateral loans: loans secured by chattel mortgages on personal property or other assets.[3]

Friends and Relatives

These are sources that should not be overlooked, although caution should be taken when borrowing from such people. Some beautiful friendships have been ruined over borrowed money. Also, friends and relatives will often want some equity in the business, that is, part-ownership which enables them to share in the profits. It is preferable to avoid equity financing because you may find that you don't have total control over how the business is conducted. It is much better to sign a promissory note, if required, specifying the terms of repayment, including the repayment period and the rate of interest.

Partnerships

The basic financial difference between a corporation and a partnership is that the officers of a corporation are not responsible for the corporation's debts, while in a partnership the partners are. If a corporation declares bankruptcy, creditors are entitled to first payment from the corporation's assets. Bondholders are next, followed by holders of preferred stock and then common stockholders. In a partnership, each partner is responsible for company debts incurred by the other partner or partners. Still, the only way to raise sufficient capital for a business may be for two or more people to form a partnership. The drawback, or course, is that if the company fails, each partner may find himself in debt for an amount exceeding his initial investment. And, of course, there will be disagreements as to how the business is run. If possible, straight partnerships should be avoided.

Limited Partnerships

A limited partnership is one in which you, as the major investor, become the general partner and run the business. If the business succeeds, the limited partners share in the profits. If the business fails, the limited partners lose only the amount they invested. They are not responsible for company debts. The drawback to this arrangement is that you do all the work without realizing 100 percent of the profits. The money is interest-free, however, and doesn't have to be paid back until you sell the business. If you're thinking of such an arrangement, be sure to consult a lawyer.

Second Mortgage on Your Home

If you own your house and have for some time, you might be able to borrow against the equity you have in it. Inflation has recently raised the market value of your home and the equity you have in it is the current market value less the amount you still owe on the original mortgage. One disadvantage is that the bank might insist on remortgaging the amount still owed. If you bought the house some time ago, you will have to pay a much higher interest rate on that amount than when you closed on the house. Also, in the early years of a mortgage, a very small portion of the monthly payments is applied against the principal; most of each payment is for interest. So it will take a longer time to rebuild your equity.

Insurance Policies

If you own either a paid-up or straight life policy, as opposed to term insurance, these policies have been building a cash value. Usually, you can borrow against this cash value at relatively low interest rates and with no specified repayment schedule. The disadvantage is that you may be providing insufficient security for your family. There are usually tables in the policy itself which will show cash values for various periods of time. Or call your agent.

Private Capital

You can run a small classified ad in the business section of a large newspaper or in the *Wall Street Journal*. The headline might read "Cash Wanted," followed by a very brief description of the use to which the money will be put. If it is for a well-known franchise, be sure to say so. There are many people with money to invest who read these ads, although they may demand relatively high rates of interest.

Finance Companies

These companies will often provide loans when banks will not, and often for longer periods of time. They will, also, often accept as collateral items unacceptable to banks. The interest rate, however, will be quite high. It is also possible that if you wish to pay the loan before the agreed-upon date you will not receive a reduction in the total long-term interest amount.

Factors

This is a fairly new method used in financing franchises, but one which has become quite prominent.

It works simply. The new franchisee receives the full amount of money needed to purchase kitchen equipment, furniture, fixtures, machinery . . . whatever durable goods are required. Instead of having to raise the capital needed to purchase such items outright, the franchisee agrees to make monthly payments over a period of from about three to as many as twenty years.

Many different types of investors are now involved in such leaseback arrangements. Universities and pension funds are involved, and there are also companies which specialize in leasing real estate and equipment to franchisees. Many of the latter are subsidiaries of franchisors.

In long-term arrangements, particularly if real estate or a building are involved, the franchisee will often have to agree to pay a fixed percentage of gross sales as rent. This makes the lease inflation-proof to the investor because as price goes up, so does the rent. Also, the holder of the lease owns the property and, if the company fails, can recoup the investment by selling the property.

For additional information on leasing, write to the International Franchise Association. The association's address can be found in Chapter 8.

Veterans' Loans

If you are a veteran who was on duty on or after August 5, 1964, you may qualify for an Economic Opportunity loan of up to $50,000, with repayments for as long as fifteen years. The process involved is simpler than in other forms of government borrowing and usually works in conjunction with Small Business Administration loans. Contact any Economic Opportunity or Small Business Administration office in your vicinity for details.[4] Other types of loans for veterans of either World War II or the Korean War are also available. Call or write to your nearest VA office.

Small Business Administration

The Small Business Administration can prove of immense help to a prospective franchisee, not only in assisting with loans, but also in offering information and advice. In fact, the SBA should be contacted during your preliminary studying of franchising. They have many different publications available, some free and others at a nominal cost. A phone call or letter will bring you a copy of their basic pamphlet, "SBA—What It Is. What It Does."

The SBA can provide SBA loans and Economic Opportunity loans. They license the Small Business Investment Companies (SBIC) and MESBICs (see page 85). They also sponsor SCORE (Service Corps of Retired Executives), which can provide management advice. In addition, SBA offers management courses, conferences, workshops and clinics.

If you are turned down for a loan by a bank, contact the SBA. In fact, the SBA cannot help to finance a business unless you have been turned down by a bank. Because the SBA does not know you or your background as well as your local bank does, the loan application will probably be even more demanding than that of a bank. If the SBA does not have the funds to advance, it will recommend a participating bank that will grant the loan with the SBA's guarantee.

Another way in which the SBA can assist a franchisee is through the SBA lease guarantee program. A lease guarantee is an insurance policy, issued on behalf of the small businessman, which assures his landlord that rent payments on the lease will be paid. Any small businessman eligible for an SBA loan can qualify for an SBA lease guarantee. It is usually written by a private insurance company and is backed by SBA reinsurance agreements. If a private insurance company cannot be found to participate, the SBA might occasionally guarantee the lease directly.

SBICs

SBICs are small business investment companies, privately owned, which are licensed by the Small Business Administration. The funds available for loans to small businesses consist of both private and government money. Interest rates, while competitive, will be slightly higher than bank rates. For additional information, write to:

National Association of Small Business Investment Companies
537 Washington Building
Washington, D.C. 20402

Minority Enterprise Small Business Investment Companies

MESBICs are now officially named Section 301 (D) = SBIC. They are similar to SBICs in that they, too, are privately owned, privately managed venture capital corporations. MESBICs can be incorporated in any state but can do business outside their state, anywhere in the United States. MESBICs are also subsidized by the federal government but must invest their money or lend money to businesses that are at least 50.1 percent owned by disadvantaged individuals.

MESBICs can offer assistance to small businesses, including franchises, in one of four ways:

1. The MESBIC may invest as a limited partner or by either common or prefered stock in the business.

2. The MESBIC may make a direct loan to the business at interest rates limited to state usury rates or 15 percent simple interest, whichever is lower.

3. The MESBIC may guarantee up to 100 percent of a loan from any third party.

4. The MESBIC may provide management and technical assistance for a fee. Such assistance can include financial consulting, bookkeeping, accounting, legal assistance, or advice on marketing or advertising.

Current sponsors of MESBICs include such large corporations as General Motors, Bank of America, ITT, Rockwell, Exxon, Sun Oil, and Chase Manhattan Bank. Other sponsors include religious groups, universities, foundations, individuals, and even franchise companies.

In a private interview, James H. Marx, chief of Capital Development, and Lonnie Murray, now acting chief, stated that MESBICs are great for franchisee financing. They said:

It's the vertical or horizontal integration of a business where the person says, "This is a way for me to get McDonald's in the inner city, or it's the way I could get some people to work with me as major distributors." SBA licensed a MESBIC about a month ago and the people involved are going to devote their whole program to rug cleaning. The rug cleaning business is the placement of rug cleaning machines in supermarkets and other stores ... you go in and rent them for a day for ten dollars, or whatever it is. It's been a very successful franchise operation. We see this as a means of leveraging that out further. And I guess we have a lot more in that category of people who are just expanding their own business horizons and they anticipate having some say in the operation of those businesses, not voting control, but some say in how they are operating. They're going to really use their expertise to make these other people successful, realizing that if they're successful, the payments back into MESBIC will make the investment worthwhile. [5]

For more information on MESBICs, write to:

U.S.Department of Commerce
Minority Business Development Agency
Washington, D.C. 20230

or your nearest Small Business Administration office. They will put you in touch with the MESBIC closest to you.

Summary and Conclusion

The most important step in financing your business is an accurate determination of start-up costs and how much working capital is required to run your business until the break-even point is reached and you turn a profit. In addition, allowance must be made for living expenses until your business can provide sufficient personal income. While a franchisor might offer assistance in preparing such figures, it is up to you to confirm that they are accurate. It could be most unpleasant to find yourself in business,with loan commitments made, without sufficient funds to cover personal and business costs, including loan repayments.

While studying franchising, take advantage of the many excellent publications available from government sources, including information on financing, from the SBA, VA, and the Internal Revenue Service. The knowledge acquired from these sources, in addition to that gained from other forms of study, will help you to determine the type of franchise you should consider.

Most franchisors will discourage partnerships, and many advise against equity financing, that is, obtaining funds by selling ownership shares in the business. If you must borrow money, it is better to obtain it by debt financing. Once the loans are repaid, the net profits are entirely yours.

Applying for a loan takes preparation. You must sell yourself, your financial stability, your knowledge of the business you have chosen, and your creditworthiness.

Leave yourself enough time to investigate as many loan sources as possible. In today's economic climate, interest rates are high, and you can reduce the cost of your loan by a sizeable amount if you can shop for the best terms.

Remember that a loan, like the franchise contract, is a commitment.

Franchising and the Law

The Environment before 1970

Lawmakers rarely anticipate. The history of legislation is one in which laws have been passed to *correct* injustices or what has been considered foul play. Only when enough people complain loudly enough and long enough over what they consider an intolerable situation do the wheels of our legislative systems begin to turn.

The laws that, until recently, have had any direct bearing on franchising were all passed under such circumstances. The Sherman Anti-Trust Act was passed in 1890. It declared illegal any contract, combination (in form of a trust or otherwise), or conspiracy in restraint of interstate or foreign trade. The trust was an ingenious arrangement. Stockholders with voting rights in different enterprises were induced to assign shares of common stock to a board of trustees in return for dividend-bearing trust certificates. The board was thus able

Pictured is the Los Alamitos, California, franchisee for Schwinn bicycles. Schwinn played a role in a 1967 court decision concerning territorial arrangements (see page 93).

to simultaneously control these various enterprises, which many people felt should be in competition with one another. The act finally resulted in the breaking up of the Standard Oil Company and the American Tobacco Company in 1911.

The Clayton Anti-Trust Act was passed in 1914 as a supplement to the Sherman Act. It prohibited exclusive sales contracts, rebates, and local price cutting which had as its purpose the elimination of competition. It also eliminated interlocking directorates in corporations in the same field of business and capitalized at one million dollars or more.

In 1936, Congress passed the Robinson-Patman Act, which forbids any person or firm engaged in interstate commerce to discriminate in price to different purchasers of the same commodity when the effect would be to lessen competition or to create a monopoly. Specifically, the act made it illegal to discriminate in price to large and small wholesalers. Often called the Chain Store Act, the purpose of the act was to protect the small retailer from chain store competition.

While the purpose of these well-intentioned acts was to prevent monopolies, the effect of much of this legislation was to limit competition, while it tended to equalize the conditions under which large and small retailers do business.

A word need be said about the Federal Trade Commission (FTC). Established in 1914 by the Federal Trade Commission Act, its duties are, in general, to promote fair competition through enforcement of antitrust laws and to prevent deceptive practices. It has the authority to issue cease-and-desist orders. It was also given the responsibility of investigating the workings of business in general and to keep Congress and the public informed of practices and situations that may call for further legislation.

In addition to these laws, the Lanham Act of 1946 requires the licensors of a trademarked product or service to exercise control over the licensee to ensure that the quality of that product or service is as advertised. If the quality is not as advertised, the franchisor risks the loss of the trademark.

If some of these laws seem contradictory, you are right. The franchisor must tread a fine line to satisfy both the antitrust laws and to protect a trademark.

Until 1970, this was the legal background under which franchising grew in the American economy.

The Constitution of the United States gives to Congress the power to regulate interstate commerce. That means that a franchisor that operates in only one state is not subject to federal statutes or to FTC rulings and regulations. If a state's business laws were weak, unscrupulous franchisors operating only in that state faced few restrictions in promoting and selling franchises. Even when involved in interstate commerce, the absence of federal rules and laws specifically covering franchising made it much easier for dishonest and fraudulent operators to prey upon gullible, unsophisticated investors. Finally, complaints from the abused had their effect and both the states and the federal government became involved.

The U.S. Senate began an investigation and the report of the Select Committee on Small Business, released in 1970, said:

"Sufficient evidence has been presented to the committee to support the conclusion that dishonest and unscrupulous practices have been employed by a segment of the franchising industry."[1]

The committee felt that full-disclosure legislation was required at the federal level and that franchisors should provide complete and detailed information on the proposed franchise relationship to prospective franchisees.

A year later, the first state law specifically covering franchising was passed.

State Laws

In 1971, California became the first state to pass a franchise law. Its basic provision is that any franchisor wishing to do business in the state must register with the state and comply with full-disclosure requirements before any franchise agreement can be signed.

This was followed by the passage of similar laws in other states and today there are fifteen states with franchise laws. As these laws are not identical, the franchisors wishing to sell franchises on a multistate basis were faced with expenditures of thousands of dollars, to say nothing of their time, to comply with the many different disclosure requirements. Recognizing this, the International Franchise Association sought to work out a system of uniform compliance procedures with a number of state administration officials. Finally, the Uniform Franchise Offering Circular (UFOC) was agreed upon, and today a total of fourteen states have adopted UFOC and its guidelines, with certain modifications, in administering their franchise registration and disclosure laws.[2]

While adoption of UFOC has simplified compliance procedures for franchisors in these states, there is still the problem of complying with a great variety of laws in those states which have neither franchise laws nor disclosure-of-information requirements. Many of these states apply so-called "little Federal Trade Commission acts" and "Unfair Practices acts" in dealing with franchise irregularities.[3]

Compounding this situation are "Blue Sky laws," which have been enacted by about half the states. Under these laws, corporations wishing to do business in a state must register with securities administrators. In considering a registration application, the state must find that the investment opportunity is "fair, just and equitable." Such language is far from precise and, even when there are guidelines, franchisor applications are subject to the judgments of state officials.

California, in 1978, proposed a new form of regulation to tie in with its Blue Sky law. Under the proposal, every franchisor seeking to sell franchises in the state would have to prove that the major elements of his franchise contract, disclosure statement, policies, and practices were "fair, just, and equitable." "Failure to sustain such proof could result in denial or suspension of registration, plus, possibly, a lawsuit by a franchisee."[4]

California has also suggested proposals that would limit fees, prices of products which franchisees are required to purchase from either the franchisor or its designated suppliers, and termination and renewal policies.[5]

Without going into too much detail here, the International Franchise Association has submitted serious objections to the proposal. One of its major objections is that the California Corporation Department, which administers the state's franchise laws, would have excessive powers and the authority to make judgmental decisions in areas that are now the responsibilities of the courts. There is the objection, too, that the commission seeks to exercise its authority beyond disclosure to "the continuing franchise relationship"—or "the entire franchise contract."[6]

Other states are constantly revising laws, and the prospects are for continuing ferment in the field of state laws and regulations.

Federal Regulatory Action

Almost ten years after the report of the U.S. Senate Select Committee on Small Business, "Impact of Franchising on Small Business," the FTC issued a rule entitled "Disclosure Requirements and Prohibitions Concerning Franchising and Business Opportunity Ventures." A copy of the Franchise Rule Summary, as released by the FTC on December 21, 1978, is included in Appendix C, page 142.

It should be emphasized that while an FTC regulation has considerable force, it is not the same as statutory law. The FTC exists only with the consent of Congress. Under political pressure and assaults by lobbyists, Congress can limit the commission's authority to issue rulings or to enforce its regulations. As this book is being written, in the summer of 1980, the two Houses of Congress are pitted against each other over a one-House veto provision in a proposed new FTC reauthorization bill.

Whatever language finally emerges in new legislation, the commission and other regulatory agencies have been alerted to the fact that their authority, especially as it relates to legislative powers, is under closer scrutiny than ever.

At this time, however, the commission's franchise rule has the same effect as a law. Under this rule, there is finally a nationwide federal regulation which applies to the sale of franchises.

Because of the importance of this rule, the FTC published a question and answer pamphlet which has helped to explain its most important points. It reads as follows:

Q. *What is a Trade Regulation Rule?*
A. *A Trade Regulation Rule sets basic standards for lawful business conduct. A Trade Regulation Rule may be issued by the Commission to prevent unfairness or deception in business dealings either by prohibiting certain acts and practices or by imposing affirmative obligations, such as disclosure of pertinent information.*

Q. *What will this Rule do?*
A. *The Rule will require sellers of franchises and other business opportunity ventures to provide prospective investors with the information they need to make an informed investment decision. It will further protect investors by requiring that all earnings claims be documented, that the information investors receive is complete and accurate, and that they have adequate time to consider and evaluate the disclosures before making any final commitment.*

Q. *Who will be covered by this Rule?*
A. *The Rule is designed to cover sellers of franchises and business opportunity ventures. Generally speaking, it will apply to the sale of franchises of an entire retail business (e.g., a fast-food restaurant) and of distribution rights for trademarketed products (e.g., an automobile dealership), as well as such business opportunity ventures as vending machine route programs. Businesses will, of course, need to compare their marketing arrangements with the Rule's definition of the types of franchises which are covered to determine whether they must comply with the Rule. The Commission staff is available for assistance in this regard.*

Q. *What penalties will a franchisor or franchise broker face for violating this Rule?*

A. *The penalties are substantial. The Commission will ordinarily be able to seek civil penalties of up to $10,000 a day for each violation of the Rule and may seek to enjoin continued violations. The Commission, also, may be able to seek additional relief in some cases.*

Q. *What prompted the Commission to issue the Rule?*
A. *The Commission began this rulemaking proceeding after receiving a significant number of consumer complaints about franchise and business opportunity venture sales practices. The rulemaking record alone contains over 5,400 pages of consumer complaint letters. Although the complaints covered many subjects, the root cause of the complaints was the same—the unavailability of reliable information essential for investors to make informed investment decisions and to verify the claims made by franchise salespersons.*

Q. *What kind of public participation went into the formulation of the Rule?*
A. *Public interest and participation in the rulemaking process has been substantial and widespread. The rulemaking record contains more than 5,400 pages of letters from consumers, some 5,000 pages of comment from state and federal government agencies and members of the academic community. It also includes almost 2,000 pages of transcript from public hearings on the Rule.*

Q. *What is the time frame for implementation and enforcement of the Rule?*
A. *The Rule published today (December 21, 1978) will take effect on July 21, 1979. The proposed implementation guidelines which accompany the Rule will be open for public comment until February 20, 1979, and will be published in final form before the effective date of the Rule.*

Q. *Does the Rule provide for consumer refunds? Does it give investors the right to sue for violations?*
A. *The Rule expressly requires that any refunds promised by the seller of a franchise or business opportunity venture be made. The Commission can sue to obtain appropriate relief for investors injured by a violation of a Rule. Although there is some question about whether federal courts will permit individual investors to sue for relief from a Rule violation, the Commission has publicly stated its view that private actions would add a valuable dimension to its own enforcement efforts. Even if the Commission's view is not adopted by courts at the federal level, investors may be able to obtain relief from state courts under State "Baby FTC Acts" and common law.*

Q. *What type of enforcement actions can be expected from the Commission?*
A. *We plan an active program of educating sellers of franchises and other business opportunity ventures about their compliance obligations, monitoring their compliance efforts, and proceeding against those who fail to comply.*

Q. *Will the Rule supersede State law?*
A. *The Rule will supersede only those few State franchise disclosure law provisions which provide less protection by investors. By setting minimum nationwide disclosure standards, the Rule should encourage individual states to continue to take an active regulatory role in providing even greater protection to investors.*

Q. *What steps should a would-be investor take before investing in a franchise or other business opportunity venture?*
A. *We recommend five basic precautions:*
1. Study the required disclosure statement and proposed contracts carefully.
2. Consult with an attorney and other professional advisors before making a binding commitment.
3. Be sure that all promises made by the seller or its salespersons are clearly written into the contracts you sign.

4. Talk with others who have already invested in the business. Find out about their experiences.

5. If you are relying on any earnings claims or guarantees, study the statements describing the basis of the claims. Find out the percentage of past investors who have done equally well.

The rule establishes the types of information about the franchisor, or a franchise broker, which must be provided in a disclosure statement. In all, twenty different topics are covered, including information about the franchisor, the business the franchisor represents, and the terms of the franchise agreement.

Information about the franchisor must include a description of the business experience of the franchisor's directors and key executives, the business experience of the franchise company, and a history of litigation and bankruptcy, if any, of both the franchise company and the directors and key executives.

The franchise must be thoroughly described and the amount of money, if any, required to obtain franchise rights must be clearly stated, as must the amount of continuing expenses that the franchisee must pay to the franchisor in operating the business. Also listed must be the names of any other parties with whom the franchisee must or is advised to do business.

Financial assistance, franchise restrictions, site selection, training programs, and participation of the franchisee are all topics which must be covered.

If the franchisor makes a representation about earnings, it must have a reasonable basis, be prepared according to generally accepted accounting principles, and be backed by substantiating evidence. Such evidence must be made available to both the FTC and the prospective franchisee upon reasonable demand. Furthermore, such a representation of earnings must be given to the prospective franchisee on either the first personal meeting with the franchisor or at least ten days prior to the execution of a contract or payment relating to the franchise relationship. This same condition holds for the disclosure statement and a copy of the franchisor's standard franchise agreement.

It is important to realize that this FTC rule sets minimum standards. In those cases where state requirements do not meet such minimum standards, the FTC format must be followed. If the requirements of a state exceed those of the FTC rule, then the state's standards may take precedence.

The preceding highlights major provisions of the FTC rule. Complete disclosure requirements are included in the Franchise Rule Summary, which is reprinted in Appendix C, page 142.

The basic complaint addressed by the FTC ruling was the lack of reliable information needed by a prospective franchisee in studying franchisor proposals. The setting of minimum standards, if enforced, takes the prospective franchisee out of the dark and into the light in the decision-making process.

Under the federal rule and under some of the state laws, there is no requirement that the disclosure statement be prefiled or registered with any regulatory authority. Where such registration is not required, it is wise for the prospective franchisee to validate the reliability of the information disclosed. In some states where registration is required, there are even exemptions for large franchisors with a substantial net worth (usually $5,000,000), for those which have had a number of franchises operating for at least five years, or have continuously operated the business for five consecutive years. So, in evaluating a franchise opportunity, it is perfectly reasonable that you seek confirmation of the information on a franchisor's disclosure document with the appropriate state authority.

While disclosure statements certainly make life easier for a prospective franchisee, they do not guarantee that a franchise will be successful once a contract is signed. Disclosure statements present information only; the franchisee and his lawyer must still determine if contract terms are reasonable.

There are, however, other federal and state laws which regulate certain aspects of a franchise contract, and these topics should be studied separately.

Franchise Termination Issues

The FTC ruling has no control over franchise terminations except that the reasons for it be included in the disclosure statement. Many states, however, recognizing that a franchisee makes a considerable investment in his business, have passed laws which protect the franchisee from arbitrary and wrongful termination on the part of the franchisor. A listing of these states is in Appendix D, page 144.

Congress has also been studying this issue, and while passage of legislation has been delayed, it is highly likely that a federal law regulating termination will be on the books in the near future. "Termination has been upheld for failure to meet sales quotas, failure to observe quality standards, and to protect franchisors from liability arising from the franchisee's acts, or other acts of misconduct."[7]

Territorial Exclusivity

Most franchisees like territorial exclusivity, and it is a very important element in many franchise agreements. Often referred to as "vertical" exclusivity, it is a marketing tool which many franchisors consider a major component of a successful marketing strategy. The justification for exclusivity, contend franchisors, is twofold. It enables the franchisor to, first, "limit and protect the franchisee's area of operation and, second, to assure that the franchisee will maintain the quality of the franchisor's product or service and the goodwill associated with his name or trademark."[8]

It has long been held by the courts that dividing up a territory or geographical area among competing sellers is a clear violation of antitrust laws. The matter becomes more complicated when a manufacturer or franchisor establishes exclusive territories for distribution, retail outlets, or franchisees. There have been arguments pro and con, based on "economic justification" and the "rule of reason" test.

In the 1967 Schwinn Bicycle case, the courts held that Schwinn was in per se violation of antitrust laws because franchisees were not permitted to sell bicycles to other, nonfranchised retailers and because, in supplying bicycles to the distributors, the manufacturer had given up title to the goods.

A per se violation is one in which any territorial arrangement, regardless of economic justification, is in violation of antitrust laws. The rule of reason approach considers all factors before deciding whether an unreasonable restraint has been imposed. Where the rule of reason is applied, it is up to the marketer to prove that competition has not been lessened by the territorial arrangement.

This is exactly what happened in the 1977 General Telephone and Electronics Sylvania case. Because Sylvania allowed distributors to sell television sets to any other party and because the territories were established with the consent of franchisees, the Supreme Court overruled the per se ruling made in the Schwinn decision.

Sources of Supply

A tie-in is an arrangement whereby a business is required to take on some product or products, even if not desired, in order to get a desired product. The courts have long recognized the rights of businessmen to purchase supplies from any source and generally condemn practices such as tying as clearly in violation of antitrust laws.

Federal trademark laws, however, require the owner of a trademark to preserve the quality of the goods or services marketed under that trademark. A trademark licensing arrangement, as in franchise agreements, is therefore not necessarily in violation of antitrust laws. The key factor is that such arrangements should not be intended to reduce competition.

Nor do the courts look favorably upon a manufacturer's or franchisor's attempt to dictate third-party suppliers. In the *Siegal v Chicken Delight* case, the franchisor pointed out that although franchisees were required to purchase all supplies and equipment from designated suppliers, there were no royalties or franchise fee. The defense also contended that "The Chicken Delight System" was actually a single product; that the alleged tie-in was really an accounting device which compensated the franchisor for allowing the use of the trademark; and that damages, if any, should be reduced by a "reasonable value" for the Chicken Delight license.

The courts of California rejected all defenses, holding that a franchise is marketable separate and apart from various products which must be purchased from or through the franchisor. The courts distinguished between a franchise system which distributes trademarked goods and those that conduct a business under a common trademark or trade name. Chicken Delight, in other words, was not marketing a trademarked product and, therefore, even in the absence of a franchise fee or royalties, was tying in products with the franchise license.

When designating suppliers, a franchisor must prove that such an arrangement is absolutely necessary to protect the trademark and the quality of the products or services it represents. In certain cases, the courts have permitted the designation of suppliers as long as any other vendor is given the chance to prove that it can meet the standards and specifications and thus become an approved vendor.

Resale Price Fixing

If a manufacturer or trademark owner attempts to control the price by which his product or service is resold to the public, it is a per se violation of the antitrust laws. It is permissible for a franchisor to suggest a retail price, but if there is any coercion or a penalty for not pricing the product as suggested, the entire franchise agreement may be judged as illegal.

Attorney Stanley B. Bernstein states:

One who seeks to adopt a franchise program as part of a marketing plan without being aware of the legal do's and don'ts represented by this ever-increasing body of law is as foolish as one seeking to float a raft upstream against the rapids. The regulations are not designed to prevent or restrict, and if approached properly do not hinder franchising programs. The laws are designed to eliminate abuses and to place franchisors and franchisees on an equal footing.

Franchising involves the creation of a partnership between two entrepreneurs—the franchisor, who has developed the system, and the franchisee, who is being asked to make a personal commitment of capital, time and effort as an independent businessman in that system.

The laws and rules governing the sale of franchises are designed to provide the prospective franchisee with the type of information one would desire to have in order to make an informed investment decision. They are designed to answer the four basic questions:

—With whom am I going into business?
—What is it going to cost me? Initially?
  During the relationship?
—What am I going to get for my money?
—What can I expect to receive as a return on my investment?

The laws and rules require full and complete disclosure on the part of the franchisor, prior to the passing of money or the making of any commitments, as to the business and personal history of key persons involved on the part of the franchisor, the description of the franchise, the franchisor's financial position, the initial and recurring costs to be paid by the franchisee, what benefits the franchisor is offering, and details about existing franchises.

The laws and rules governing the relationship recognize that the franchisee as an independent entrepreneur desires, like any other person who owns his or her business, to build equity which can be sold or passed on to his or her heirs. Accordingly, these laws and rules preclude a franchisor from terminating a franchise relationship except for "good cause" and require that, unless "good cause" exists, franchise agreements be renewed after the expressed expiration date.

Acceptance of the fact that a franchisee is a partner—not an employer—of a franchisor should be easy. The success of a franchise system depends on the ability to have successful and profitable outlets. Thus, from a business viewpoint the system must be structured so as to permit the franchisee to make a reasonable return on investment, and from a legal viewpoint it must be structured so as to make certain that a proper investor is obtained and that he or she is in a position to retain or maximize the profits he or she makes.

As much care should be given to the proper preparation of the program, the necessary disclosure documents, financial statements, and the franchise agreement, as to the development of the components of the franchise system and the marketing thereof.[9]

The Elusive Definition of Franchise

Fundamental to any laws on franchising is a standard definition of what constitutes a franchise. The FTC rule "is designed to cover sellers of franchises and, also, business opportunity ventures." The rule lists three characteristics of each of two types of franchises and then lists seven exemptions. It also covers relationships "which are represented as being written the definition (of franchise) when the relationship is entered into, regardless of whether, in fact, they are within the definition."

In a booklet entitled "Franchise Law Summary,"[10] Vernon Haas takes eleven pages to describe all the considerations involved in determining whether or not a business is a franchise under California law.

Michael J. Brody, acting assistant commissioner of the Department of Corporations in the State of California, had the following to say about franchise definitions:

It would be to the benefit of all franchisors and franchisees and consumers if we had a Uniform Franchise Registration which would include franchises as commercial transactions under the Uniform Commercial Code. Legislative sanctions against pyramid and promo-

Franchising and the Law

tional schemes that are inherently fraudulent and deceptive should not be tarred with the same brush as the ethical franchisors. State and federal regulators should define more clearly what is—and what is not—a franchise. [11]

It should be clear from Mr. Brody's statement that a clear definition of franchising would be advantageous to both franchisors and franchisees in more than just a legal sense.

In a legal sense, however, it is obvious that the relationship between an automobile manufacturer and a dealer who sells his product is different from that between a franchisor and, for instance, a fast-food restaurant which prepares the product sold. And certainly a soft-drink bottler is not in the same business as a franchisee who provides a bookkeeping or tax preparation service.

For the benefit of all those involved in franchising, including the courts, a clear, comprehensive definition of franchise would do much to improve the current environment of uncertainty.

Summary and Conclusion

The purpose of this chapter has not been to make you an expert in the field of franchise law. Far from it. There is still much to be done in our legislative systems to clarify the laws that already exist and to provide further protection for franchisees with additional laws or amendments that do not unreasonably inhibit franchisors.

Disclosure laws in some states and the FTC rule on franchising does much to prevent fraudulent representations by unscrupulous, quick-buck operators or those that represent themselves as franchisors but really are not. Such disclosure requirements are another valuable tool which can be used in evaluating franchise opportunities. Because the FTC rule and some of the state laws do not mandate prefiling of disclosure statements, it is wise to check the laws of the state in which you seek a franchise. If prefiling is not required, there is no reason why you should not submit the disclosure statement to the appropriate state authorities to see if it has been prepared in accordance with franchise laws and regulations. Your tax money pays these people's salaries, and you certainly are entitled to their time.

Beware of the franchisor who insists in the contract that you not join a franchisor association. Collective action is usually much more effective than individual action, and if a franchise association is large enough it should have the funds to retain a lawyer to protect the interests of all those involved. Remember, too, that any attempt to dictate the selling price of the franchisor's products or services is probably illegal.

In the absence of a franchise law, the statutes that apply to your contract are primarily the antitrust laws. Most of these laws were passed in an effort to curb monopolies and to encourage competition. If it seems that a provision of the franchise agreement would restrict competition, it is possible, though not certain, that it is also illegal.

In the case of litigation, courts often rely on previous decisions that have set a precedent. The Sylvania case, however, was not the first in which a precedent set by one court has not been applied by another. Nor was it the last. Court trials can be extremely expensive and time-consuming. Some cases involving major corporations have dragged on for five years or more. In a very complex situation, it may be advisable to settle out of court, even if the prospects are for an eventual favorable decision. The best defense, of course, is not to have to go to court at all.

Once again, it is advised that a prospective franchisee make use of a competent lawyer. The services of a good lawyer can run from about $40 to $125 an hour, but such a fee is well worth it. (By the way, negotiate the lawyer's fee, too.) But don't wait until you have a problem after a franchise agreement has been signed. You can save yourself a lot of grief if a lawyer is consulted before the contractual commitment is made.

Where to Learn More about Franchising

In addition to the books which have been written about franchising, there are many other good sources of information. Some of these are devoted exclusively to franchising; others are on the subject of small business in general. As the franchisee is a small entrepreneur, much of this latter material can be very helpful to both the prospective franchisee or the one already in business. There are periodicals devoted to small business, annual franchise directories and many newsletters and pamphlets. If you're fortunate enough to live near a good library, you can save yourself time and money in researching the subject thoroughly. The U.S. Government is also an extremely good source.

Here are the details on each of these sources:

Federal Government

Each month the federal government publishes the "Monthly Catalogue of United States Government Publications." This lists all the publica-

Where to Learn More about Franchising

tions written and compiled by the various agencies and departments of the federal government. All you have to do to get this is to write to:

Superintendent of Documents
Washington, D.C. 20402

Ask that you be put on the mailing list. The catalogue is free.

You'll find that the contents are indexed three ways: by subject, by author, and by title. Initially, you'll probably do best by consulting the subject index under the categories "Business," "Small Business," and "Franchising."

Many government publications are free; others are available at a nominal cost. Instructions on ordering any of the publications listed are included in the monthly catalogue. They can be ordered through the mail order facilities of:

U.S. Government Printing Office
Washington, D.C. 20402

A listing of regional branches of printing office bookstores is also included in the catalogue. It might be possible for you to get material more quickly through one of the regional offices.

Small Business Administration   The Small Business Administration is a division of the U.S. Department of Commerce. There are eighty-nine regional offices of the SBA throughout the United States. The address and phone number of the office nearest you can be found in the Yellow Pages under United States Government. The Washington address is

Small Business Administration
Washington, D.C. 20416

The Small Business Administration can be of great help to the small business person. More information about the SBA can be obtained by requesting a free copy of SBA—What it is. What it does.

The SBA has produced a host of publications dealing with small business. Among these are "Small Business Bibliographies," a reference source for business owners and managers and prospective small business people, and "Small Marketers Aids," guides for retail, whole-sale, and service firms.

Other publications are the "Small Business Management" series. There is also a "Starting and Managing" series and a "Small Business Research" series.

Some booklets of specific interest which I find to be very good for the prospective franchisee are

GPO 864–519	Focal Points on Franchising
OPI 15	SBA-Bank Participation Loans— Purchase of SBA Loans
OPI 15	SBA Business Loans
OPI 18A	Announcing Business Loans for Veterans
SMA 71	Checklist for Going into Business
SMA 35	Franchise Index Profile
SMA 106	Finding and Hiring the Right Employees
SMA 154	Using Census Data to Select a Site

Federal Trade Commission   For a free copy of "Advice for Persons Who Are Considering an Investment in a Franchise Business," write to the Government Printing Office or

Federal Trade Commission
6th St. and Pennsylvania Avenue, N.W.
Washington, D.C. 20580

Also of interest is "Franchise Business Risks" (Consumer Bulletin No. 4).

Department of Commerce   The Department of Commerce is another excellent source of material on franchising. The department's Industry and Trade Administration publishes very helpful statistical data and the Office of Minority Business Enterprise (OMBE) operates six regional and twelve field offices to assist minority groups in small business matters.

Two publications of value to a franchise or prospective franchise are *The Franchise Opportunities Handbook* and "Franchising in the Economy." These can be ordered through the government printing office or

United States Department of Commerce
Industry and Trade Administration
Washington, D.C. 20402

The Franchise Opportunities Handbook is published annually and provides a current listing of nondiscriminatory franchisors and vital information about each. While the information on each franchisor is not nearly as complete as that required in a disclosure statement, it can be very useful in evaluating franchise opportunities. The *Handbook* also gives the addresses of OMBE regional and field offices as well as addresses of private, nonprofit business development organizations with which the department is affiliated. The latter organizations can be especially helpful to members of minority or disadvantaged groups.

"Franchising in the Economy" is published periodically. The booklet covering the 1977–1979 period provided much statistical data for this book. There is also a short text which discusses recent developments and other areas of interest to both the prospective and the current franchisee.

For additional information on franchisors, request a copy of

CPO 609-201   Franchise Company Data

Other Government Agencies   The Internal Revenue Service publishes two excellent booklets for the small business person. They are

Pub. 454   Mr. Businessman's Kit

Pub. 334   The Tax Guide for Small Business

The Department of Labor has published "Want to be Your Own Boss?" This is free and can be obtained by writing to

Department of Labor
Washington, D.C. 20210

State Government

In analyzing costs to run a business, you should take into consideration state tax requirements for both the business and your employees.

Where to Learn More about Franchising

Some states offer special tax incentives for new, small businesses and you should certainly take advantage of such programs if they exist.

Look in the Yellow Pages for the appropriate state office. All state offices are usually listed under the name of the state. For example, if you live in New York, the proper heading in the phone book is New York State.

Libraries

If you happen to live near a good library, you should take advantage of the many fine services it can provide. The librarian should be able to help you in finding material on franchising or small business. If you live near a university or college, you should inquire there. Some colleges with business schools have excellent business libraries, and some are open to the public. There are also other libraries which specialize in business subjects, particularly in big cities. You'll have to do some investigating to find out where they are.

If you have trouble finding a good business library, there is a special directory that might be of help. It is called *The Directory of Special Libraries* and is published by Gale Research Company of Detroit, Michigan. Periodic supplements are published to keep it up to date. Unfortunately, the libraries are listed alphabetically instead of geographically. However, the directory provides information about each library, including size, number of volumes, and the name of the head librarian. The library nearest you might have it as a reference book. It can be a valuable tool if you don't mind spending a little time to find what you're looking for.

Franchise Directories

In addition to *The Franchise Opportunities Handbook*, published annually by the U.S. Department of Commerce, other good directories are

Franchising Annual
Info Press, Inc.
Lewiston, New York 14092

Directory of Franchise Organization
Pilot Books
New York, New York 10016

Dow-Jones Irwin Guide to Franchising
Dow-Jones Irwin
Homewood, Illinois 60430

Periodicals

Magazines There are two excellent magazines that are devoted exclusively to small business. They often contain articles specifically on franchising. They are

Entrepreneur Magazine
Chase Revel, Inc.
2311 Pontius Avenue
Los Angeles, California 90064

Venture, the Magazine for Entrepreneurs
Venture Magazine
35 West 45th Street
New York, New York 10036

Newsletters There are two newsletters being published today on a monthly basis exclusively devoted to franchising. They usually run about eight pages in length and report on recent developments in the field of franchising. One is "The Info Franchise Newsletter" and the other is "Full Disclosure." The latter monitors "Disclosure Requirements and Prohibitions Concerning Franchising and Business Opportunity Ventures." Both of these are relatively expensive and might prove of more value to you after you have already become a franchisee. For subscription costs and perhaps a sample issue, write to

The Info Franchise Newsletter
736 Center Street
Lewiston, New York 14092

Full Disclosure
Business Publications Division
Rudy Haupt & Company, Inc.
231 Hay Avenue
Johnstown, Pennsylvania 15902

Seminars

The following organizations offer seminars on franchising:
New York University, New York, N.Y. American Management Association, New York, N.Y. American Marketing Association, Chicago, Ill. Growth Strategies, Inc., San Francisco, Cal. Seltz Franchising Developments, Inc., New York, N.Y. Small Business Administration, Washington, D.C. The United States Department of Commerce, Washington, D.C.

New York Management Center, Inc., New York, N.Y., is an excellent source of information on franchise seminars. Also inquire of the college or university nearest you.

Consultants

If you are genuinely serious about purchasing a franchise but feel that you need expert advice before making a decision, then it might be wise to pay for the services of a consultant. Such a consultant can best be contacted through personal recommendations from such people as a banker, lawyer, accountant, or company that uses consultants.

Other excellent sources are

Institute of Management Consultants, Inc., New York, N.Y., and Association of Management Consultants, Inc., Milwaukee, Wis. College and university business departments are other good places to seek advice on consultants. You can also look in the Yellow Pages. Look under Franchise Consultants, Business Consultants, Management Consultants, or Marketing Consultants. Talk to as many of these as you can before making a decision. Factors to consider are client served, experience and, of course, fee. Talk to other people who have used these consultants' services, if possible, before making a final decision.

Trade Associations

There are literally thousands of business, professional, and trade associations in the United States. Check first to see if there is a franchisee association that represents the type of business you are considering. You should also definitely contact the International Franchise Association.

Where to Learn More about Franchising

The IFA is an association of franchisors which imposes strict standards of ethics on its members. It can also serve as a valuable conduit of information to prospective franchisees or investors. Write to:

International Franchise Association
7513 Wisconsin Avenue
Washington, D.C. 20014

Other Literature

A number of books have been written on franchising and other literature, such as pamphlets, booklets, and studies, is also available. Many of these are included in the bibliography at the end of this book.

Odds-On Favorites for the 1980s

9

A Period of Continuing Change

Historians, sociologists, scientists, and those who attempt to forecast the future all agree on one fact—humankind has never before gone through a period of such rapid change as we are now experiencing. It took centuries for the world to change from a feudal, primarily agricultural society and proceed through the industrial revolution. But in the thirty-five years since the end of World War II, particularly among the free, industrialized nations, society has probably changed as much as it did in the previous three hundred and fifty years.

Today we are living in what Daniel Bell called the Post-Industrial Society (see Bibliography). Since the nineteenth century, the percentage of U.S. employment in manufacturing is declining. In 1947 it was about 30 percent; in 1968 it was 25 percent. The exact figure today is unimportant, the trend is evident. Automation will continue to reduce

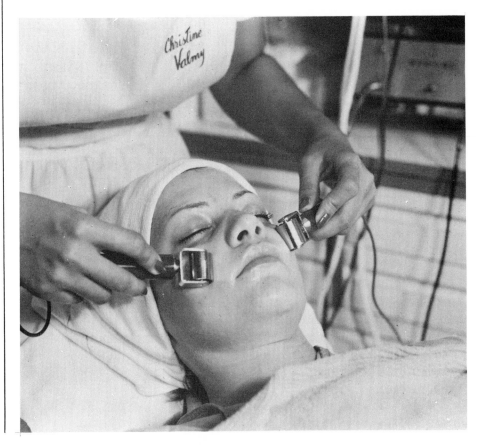

Personal care products and services may be a good bet for the 1980s. The Christine Valmy skin care salons, such as the one shown here, specialize in European methods of revitalizing skin brought to this country by the European-born Miss Valmy.

Odds-On Favorites for the 1980s

the number of those employed in manufacturing occupations.

It wasn't too many years ago that an unusual strike took place at an automobile assembly plant in a town called Lordsville. Unusual in that the strike was not over wages or benefits. The strike was led by younger workers who felt that their assembly-line work was dull, boring, repetitive, and dehumanizing. Today, much of that work is being performed by robots, and the science of robotics is just beginning to make its presence felt.

According to the World Future Society, agriculture, too, is employing fewer workers than ever before. In 1790, 90 percent of the work force was in agriculture. At the close of World War II the figure was about 10 or 11 percent. Today it is somewhere between 2 and 3 percent. And we're producing more food than ever.

Where are the rest of the workers today? In the services—insurance, banking, marketing, medicine, education, hotels, restaurants, research, and a host of others. And, yes, in government.

This is the occupational background against which we can look to the future of franchising. There are, however, many other factors. These factors are all interrelated and it is difficult to look at one while ignoring the others. If you will bear this interrelationship in mind, let's look at some of them separately.

Inflation

It comes as no surprise to hear that inflation is eating away at your pocketbook. In the last ten years, the value of the dollar has fallen by 50 percent. Your government, unable to bring expenditures into line with income, has resorted to high interest rates in an attempt to control the money supply and, it hopes, inflation. Barring a depression, there seems little likelihood that there will be a meaningful abatement in inflation rates in the near future or a return to the level of interest rates prevalent in the United States as late as the 1960s. Under such circumstances, it is far more likely that new franchisors will be offering franchises that require investments much smaller than that average of $179,000 for a Burger King franchise.

Even with the ability to raise the funds necessary for a better-known fast-food restaurant franchise, they will become increasingly more difficult to obtain. Taco-Bell and Denny's have stopped franchising and about the only way one can obtain a McDonald franchise today is to buy one from a current franchisee. Why? The franchisors want to pocket the profits for themselves. It is a trend which will probably spread, particularly among those systems owned by big corporations.

What kind of franchises will be more easily obtained? The indications are they will be in varying kinds of service businesses or, if in retailing, on a smaller scale.

The American Population Is Getting Older

During the 1980s, those in the 18- to 24-year age bracket, the once highly touted youth market, will actually decline in numbers. The biggest increase will be in the 25- to 44-year age group and there will be a sizeable increase in the number of people 65 years of age and older. Coupled with a drop in the birth rate, these changes in the make-up of our population will have a decided impact not only on society and our institutions, but also on business. There will be surplus capacity in our colleges and schools (as a matter of fact, there already is). Even though federal law now prohibits the mandatory retirement of those aged 65, economists are expressing concern over the ability of a smaller base of workers to support the social security system. But services for retirees and our senior citizens should provide new opportunities for franchisors. There will be more nursing homes which will require home services. A service that picks up and delivers prescription drugs, for example, may have great potential.

Education is another field with great possibilities for franchising. With the number of full-time college applicants declining, colleges are busily promoting adult education courses to attract the tuitions needed to remain open. Many of these are self-improvement courses or courses which enable people to learn new occupations. Can franchising contribute to this process, perhaps by providing audiovisual materials, course outlines, and inexpensive texts?

Changes in Lifestyle

These changes are with us now. The once-typical nuclear family, consisting of wife, husband, and children, with only the father working, is no longer typical. More and more mothers are working, not only because of attitudes caused by the women's movement, but because inflation is forcing them to. More couples are avoiding marriage and are simply living together. Many marrieds are delaying the birth of children or having none at all. The average family size has decreased and many mothers return to work soon after the birth of a child. On top of all this, the divorce rate has soared.

The result is a mixed bag for business. Child care services, despite a decline in the birth rate, will continue to be in demand. On the other hand, with both husband and wife working, the demand for home services should grow. Couples will continue to value their free time together and the leisure activities or entertainment businesses should remain strong. With the high cost of transportation, however, there will probably be more demand for such businesses closer to home. In home services, such businesses as upholstery and carpet cleaning, interior decoration, lawn and garden care, painting—many of those functions formerly provided by the husband or housewife—represent great opportunities for franchising.

Rapid Technological Change

Computers and data processing equipment have caused their own revolutions. Today there are firms that specialize in providing computerized services for realty property managers, travel agencies, and the medical and health fields, to name only a few.

The demand for information has never been greater, and this demand has extended beyond business to the social services and government. Office computers or time-sharing arrangements will be integral parts of the "office of the future."

Home computers, too, may prove to be big business. These can be used not only for paying bills, ordering merchandise, and handling home finances in general, but also for business purposes. Executives might spend more time at home in their own computerized offices. The possibilities for computers, or "hardware," and the "software" to feed into the computers, are almost endless.

Other technological advances are on the horizon. Who knows when a breakthrough in solar energy equipment will occur? There are now hand-held devices which enable one to detect those areas of a house that are losing heat. Energy conservation will continue to be a concern of both businesses and homeowners, offering more possibilities for franchising.

What about the electrical car? Technological advances have recently been made on batteries, and testing of new designs continues. If they ever become practical, someone is going to have to charge them.

Another point about technological advances. With more and more people and businesses using increasingly sophisticated equipment, there will be the need to have this equipment serviced and repaired. With inflation, there will be the tendency to make things last as long as possible—by everyone.

The Need for Personal Gratification

We all seem to lead hectic lives today. We rush off to work and neglect eating a good breakfast. During the day we may eat junk food on the run. Then, in a rush, it's off to the gym to keep in shape. Physical fitness is a must.

Despite the fact that the population is getting older, everyone wants to look young. Faces are being lifted and hair dyed. Men no longer have their hair cut; they have it styled. There's the feeling that we all work too hard, that we're subjected to more pressure than ever before. Therefore, when we have free time, we feel we deserve to pay special attention to ourselves.

People even plan their leisure time to fit in with busy schedules. Where both husband and wife are working there's the demand for facilities close to home or the office. Tennis courts, rollerskating rinks, miniature golf courses, handball and squash courts, health clubs are all in demand. Almost everyone, it seems, wants to be physically fit, beautiful, young looking, and entertained. Suntanning parlors, becoming ever more popular, confirm the trend.

Summary and Conclusion

The purpose of this chapter has been to add another dimension to the evaluation of franchise opportunities. Simply put, that other dimension is compatability to the changing social and business environment.

People today want speed and convenience. Fast-food restaurants are a case in point. There will probably be more drive-in or drive-through types of businesses someday.

We're living in a period of specialization. The Jack-of-all-trades is becoming a thing of the past. One need only look at the automobile repair business to see evidence of this. These specialists provide a service faster and at less cost than can the vast majority of do-it-all garages. And because many businesses specialize, customers tend to place more trust in their ability to provide reliable service.

Inflation has individuals and businesses looking for every conceivable way to cut costs and improve efficiency without affecting the quality of the products or services they provide. Equipment rental businesses should continue to do well, whether they serve individuals or businesses. So should employment agencies, particularly those that specialize in personnel with specific abilities in fields such as accounting, data processing, and word processing.

With the change in lifestyles, home services should expand. Today, for example, there are franchises in such businesses as restoring porcelain on bathtubs and stripping and restoring furniture. With rising crime, the home security business is booming.

It is important that the person considering franchising as a business opportunity keep up-to-date. Read the business or financial sections of a good newspaper. A subscription to at least one respected business magazine is inexpensive but a very worthwhile investment. Stay alert to what's going on; find out all you can about people and businesses and what they need—or might need. There is a diversity of opportunity out there.

One last thought. It is the innovator who will develop the really successful franchises in the eighties and beyond. The person with ideas, the person who fills a need. Who knows, that person might just be you. Then, instead of becoming a successful franchisee, you'll become a well-known franchisor.

Checklists for Self-Evaluation

10

Evaluating a franchise opportunity and assessing your own attitude and financial capability are best approached systematically. It is certainly unwise to commit yourself to a long-term contractural agreement without carefully analyzing *all* the factors involved. It makes no difference whether you are a novice to the business or an experienced executive.

Airline pilots with hundreds of thousands, perhaps over a million miles flown, must still perform a routine system of checks both before they take off and before they land. It makes no difference how much experience a crew has had; their assignment is too important not to take every precaution.

Going into business is a big step that is not to be taken lightly. The checklist and questionnaires that follow are designed to assist you in making a wise decision. They ask hard questions. It is urged that you think carefully about each question and answer them honestly. If you don't, you could have a financial crash landing.

Checklists for Self-Evaluation

A Final Checklist before Buying a Franchise

Before making an investment in a franchise business, the prospective franchisee will want to make sure that the franchisor is reputable and that the opportunity being offered is a viable venture.

There are several excellent sources containing appropriate information in this area and these have been condensed and edited for the purpose of presenting them as concisely and clearly as possible. Readers whose interest goes beyond this short chapter are advised to consult the footnoted sources in their entirety.

A Quick Test to Avoid Unreputable Franchisors

Much time, money, and aggravation can be saved by the prospective franchisee if he or she will answer the following questions honestly:

1. Were you promised high profits in exchange for a minimum effort?

2. Did the representative pressure you to sign the contract immediately?

3. Were you told that this was your last chance to sign and, that if you did not, the opportunity would no longer be available?

4. Did the representative refuse to answer any questions or did he refuse to give specific answers?

5. Were you told of services such as training, management assistance, etc., without specific examples of each?

6. Was the representative reluctant to give you a responsible list of references?

7. Did you feel that the representative was more interested in selling you a franchise than he was in your being successful in business?

8. Did the representative try to discourage you from having your attorney review the contract before you signed it?

In addition, it might be wise for the prospective franchisee to visit or call one of the operating franchises and talk to the owner about the business to find out:

1. Does the franchisor deliver what he promises?

2. Based on the franchisee's experience, is the franchisor competent in the business of the franchise and does the franchisee consider the company itself to be well managed and responsive to his or her needs?

If the answer to questions 1–8 is NO, and if the prospective franchisee is satisfied with the discussion with operating franchisees, then the franchisor is probably reputable and further interest is justified.[1]

Evaluating the Service/Product Offered by the Franchisor

Is the type of business you are considering (e.g., motel, restaurant, cosmetics, appliances) and the type of franchise distribution (selective product distribution or entire business system franchising) one for which you have an aptitude and strong motivation?

If a product is involved, is it stable or seasonal, is it proven, and is there a market for it generally and in the territory in which you will operate, or is it untested, speculative, or a gimmick? How long has it been on the market? Is it patented, or does it involve formulas and trade secrets not available to others?

Is the product manufactured by the franchisor or a third party? How strong and reputable is the source? Check the reliability of delivery and availability. Determine who controls product prices to you and whether these prices have been and are competitive. Is any suggested and projected selling price realistic in the light of competitive product conditions and anticipated returns? What is the competition?

Are there governmental standards and regulations governing the product/service? Does it meet the standards? Are there government restrictions on use? Are there product warrantees or guarantees? Who makes them? Are there arrangements for repair or replacements?

Is there some product/service line diversification existing or planned?[2]

Evaluating the Franchisor

A. Investigate the franchisor and its officers and directors. Determine whether there is real business experience behind the company. How long has it been in business? If you are dealing with a well-established, successful operation, less investigation may be justified.

Check the current financial condition of the franchisor. If it is publicly held, data are readily available; if not, they should be requested. Your bank, local Better Business Bureau, Dun and Bradstreet, and other sources can assist you in this area.

B. If you will require financing and must find it yourself, the franchisor's reputation, credit rating, and track record, as well as the franchisor's contact may be vital to your ability to get it.

C. Verify trademarks and trade names and that they are the ones you think they are, not merely similar.

D. How many franchisees and company-owned outlets are claimed? Seek some verification.

E. Is the franchisor carefully checking your qualifications and otherwise indicating a long-term interest, or does he appear interested only in selling quickly for the initial fee? Are you being rushed or is mutual verification encouraged? Is adequate time offered to study the contract before signing?

F. Make some effort to contact other franchisees and learn about the operation from the inside. Verify that performance generally matches promises. Franchisees will not hide complaints.

Evaluating Your Own Qualifications to Be a Franchisee

A franchisor worth your confidence will want satisfactory answers to the question of your qualifications—and you should be equally interested in self-evaluation.

Jerome L. Fels suggests the the franchisee ask himself or herself these questions:

A. Have you carefully considered whether you are qualified for the franchise offered physically, by experience, education, learning capacity in view of what is required, temperament, and financial status?

Checklists for Self-Evaluation

B. Are you anticipating, prepared for, and equipped for hard work, as well as financial risk? If you intend to have only a passive or investor's role, have you determined at the outset whether the franchisor will accept this? If so, whether adequate employees will be available to you? Can you manage others? What has your personal history been in this regard? Is supervisory employee training available if you are to be passive?

C. Do your advisers, family, and friends think you are adaptable, trainable, and generally qualified?

Most franchise contracts, especially in entire business system franchising, provide for controls reasonably necessary to protect all franchisees, the system, and its image and good will by product/service quality and uniformity standards. How do you react to such controls? Are you a "lone wolf"? If so, franchising might not be for you.

Also, please see self-evaluation quiz at the end of the chapter.

Evaluating the Training Needs and Requirement of a Franchise

The prospective franchisee should recognize that training is a very important part of the franchise arrangement and should take pains to find the answers to the following questions.

A. Is experience or training required?

B. What is the nature and extent of training? What are the costs and who pays them? In assessing training costs, determine whether there is tuition; who pays room, board, and transportation; and in the latter connection, the location of the training facilities—home office plant, in an operating unit, or both. Are any of your employees included in any training cost charge or allowance agreed upon?

C. Determine whether supplemental training will be available to cover supervisory employee turnover, whether it is required or permitted, at what cost, and who bears that cost.

D. Determine whether there will be start-up assistance by franchisor personnel on the franchised premises, immediately before and for a limited time after opening the unit, including supervision of equipment layouts and operations, and start-up and preopening promotions.

Evaluating Profit Potential

Many franchise arrangements provide excellent income-producing opportunities. Not all franchises, however, yield the fantastic profits sometimes promised. Many produce less profits than represented by franchise promoters. When deceptive promotions are involved, debts rather than profits are the usual rule.[3]

Specifically, prospective franchisees can do the following:

A. Analyze the profit projections of the franchisor. Has your accountant made a projection based on data available to him and compared it to the one submitted?

B. On what is the franchisor's projection based—on his franchisee's experience or on the operation of others, and over what period of time? Is verification available?

If the projection is based on actual past and current franchisee experience, what was the area mix and character of the locations included in the computation?

C. Compare your projected profit (plus compensation for you and your family provided in the projection if you are to work) with what you would earn if you were working elsewhere. Verify these projections with other franchisees. They are a primary source for determining whether performance matches promise in every area.

Evaluating the Financial Investment

Most franchises, especially entire business system franchises, require monetary contributions by franchisees consisting of some or all of the following (in addition to plant and equipment payments where acquired from franchisors): an initial license fee, training cost (tuition, room, board, and transportation), and on-site start-up aid and promotion charges (may be included in the license fee or in whole or part separately stated); periodic royalties or service fees and an advertising contribution (usually payable monthly or weekly and based on a specified percentage of sales receipts). Sometimes, there is a charge for centralized accounting/bookkeeping data processing services.

A. The terms "cash required," "initial cash required," "investment," "downpayment," "equity investment," mean different things in different offerings.

Sometimes "initial license fee" includes training and start-up aids and promotions; sometimes not. The understanding should be clear, the contract explicit. Don't confuse downpayment with ultimate cost. What does "fee" mean? What is payment on equipment and inventory? What are deferred payments? Make sure that you know the differences.

B. Who finances the investment-deferred balances? At what interest? If the franchisor doesn't, is help in finding financing being offered? Have you received commitments for financing before committing yourself?

C. In determining total costs, check every aspect of the deal. Do not overlook the cost of finding, buying or leasing, and improving and equipping a business location, obtaining zoning licenses for the operation at that location, and the financing costs involved.

Evaluating the Location, Territory, and Operating Facility

The following are questions that the prospective franchisee should ask regarding the territory and physical location of the proposed franchised business.

A. Is your proposed franchise for a specific business location in a particular territory? Is it confined to that one location?

As generally used, the terms "site" or "location" refer to the specific land and building from which you are to conduct business, and where a fixed location is a requirement of the system, the term "territory" is frequently used to describe the geographical area in which the site is to be located and which may be assigned to you as a protected or exclusive area.

Your lawyer will advise you on some legal limitations on the extent to which an exclusive franchise protects you. "Exclusive" or "protected" frequently means only that the franchisor will not operate a facility and will not franchise others to do business from a location in the territory.

Checklists for Self-Evaluation

B. What aid will you receive from the franchisor in site selection and how expert is it in this regard? Who is to find the site, negotiate the lease or purchase, build and equip the facility? Who is to obtain financing? If you are to find, lease, or build the facility, be certain of availability and financing before you are committed. Be certain lease terms and renewals are coextensive with those of the franchise.

Premises and layout identity may be an essential part of the system image. Are you to receive plans and specifications? Is the cost included in the initial fee?

Mutual responsibilities should be clearly stated in the franchise agreement and in preliminary agreements.

If the franchisor is not to be your lessor, can you obtain a provision in the lease that lessor will not lease to a competitor in the area?

C. If a particular territory and site are specified, on what basis were they determined? Have you checked it with your advisers as to neighborhood character and quality, traffic hours and density, and surrounding business establishments, including competitive ones and the apparent activity in them? Have you checked other franchised outlets and franchisees and compared their locations and yours in the light of the foregoing?

D. Can your territory be altered with population changes?

Evaluating Operating Practices and Controls

Prospective franchisees should understand these controls before executing the franchise agreement. Doing this will benefit both the franchisee and the franchisor by eliminating the unhappy possibility of a misunderstanding. It should be remembered that the contract should be as specific as possible in regard to these items.

A. What continuing management and assistance will you receive? Are they included in the service or royalty fee, or is there some additional charge?

B. What advertising and promotion will there be? At what level—national, regional, local? Under whose direction and control? At whose and what cost? What is the franchisor's past practice and record? What is the promise? What does the contract say?

C. Will prices to you reflect benefits of the franchisor's mass purchasing power? If so, is that purchasing power merely available, or is it mandatory that you purchase from the franchisor or his designated suppliers some or all of the items you will need? Are prices to be fair and competitive?

D. What are the bookkeeping, accounting, and reporting requirements? Are the accounting system and report forms furnished? At whose and what cost? If there is centralized, franchisor-maintained accounting and data processing, is it available or required, and at whose and what cost?

E. What are the general provisions on equipment and premises maintenance, product/service quality, and character controls? Does the contract specify or limit what you may sell? Is price control by franchisor written into the agreement?

F. Are there quotas? Are they realistic? What are the penalties for not meeting them?

G. Are facility business hours specified?

H. Do you understand the extent to which noncompliance may be a terminating default?

I. Do you really accept the premise of the franchisor that its controls and specifications are required to ensure the product/service quality, standardization, and facility identification necessary to protect all franchisees and the system integrity, image, and good will?

J. Are you mentally and tempermentally attuned to accepting such direction from others?

Evaluating the Assignment of the Franchise

Prospective franchisees should give careful consideration to the possibility of assigning the franchise they are purchasing. The following questions can be useful in determining assignability:

A. Can you sell the franchised business and assign the franchise agreement to the buyer? Is the franchise assignable to your family or may it be sold by your estate on death? There are limitations on assignment in every agreement. Know and check the specific details of the contract and of the practice of your proposed franchisor. It should be rare that a franchisor unreasonably refuses assignment to a qualified assignee.

B. Check your lease. May you assign it to any permitted assignee of the franchise?

Evaluating the Term, Renewal, and Termination Possibilities

The term of a franchise agreement and termination possibility are very important considerations. Prospective franchisees are advised to pose the following questions in an attempt to clearly define the franchisor's position on these issues.

A. Most agreements will specify a term. Check this carefully. Is there any renewal right?

B. What does the contract provide about termination? Are the defaults for which there may be termination "good cause" in your opinion? Are you entitled to notice of default and to any time to cure the default? Does franchisor have any option other than "good cause" to cancel the agreement?

C. Under what conditions and on what terms may you terminate the agreement, if at all?

D. If you must arrange your own financing, have you determined in advance if the assignment, term renewal, and termination clauses are satisfactory to your proposed lending agency or equipment lessors/sellers?

E. Does the franchisor have an option or a duty to buy any or all of your equipment, furnishings, inventory, or your entire operation in the event it terminates for good cause? If it terminates without cause on expiration of the term? If you elect not to renew or if you request renewal and are refused? What is the purchase price? Are there specific formulas to be followed or will there be appraisal or arbitration?

Checklists for Self-Evaluation

Evaluating Possible Competition with Franchisor

Most franchise contracts restrict all competing operations during the term of the franchise. They also restrict any competing activity or business after the term for a limited area and for a limited period. They restrict and prohibit revealing trade secrets at any time.

Check specific terms of the contract in this regard.

Evaluating the Franchise Contract

A. Most franchisors want you to read and understand the contract. Submit it to your attorney and accountant and discuss it with them.

Check the contract against the representations made which attracted you. Are they specifically covered? Resolve misunderstandings in advance. Your contract governs your legal relationship.

B. Some sources suggest that prospective franchisees bargain for modifications of provisions they consider undesirable, or for better terms.

There may be areas for legitimate modifications for reasons where conditions legitimately vary. Your reasonable suggestions should not be ignored. If a franchisor is entering a new area which is known to you, your suggestions, for example, about inventory, product/service, or operating hour modifications justified by special or local geographic, climate, ethnic, religious or trade association customs, rules, or practices may be of value to all parties.

However, if a franchisor is sound and ethical, he will not bargain away major essential points with all comers. If he will, why were they included in the first place?

The quality and operating control sections should be structured to preserve product/service uniformity and quality and, thus, protect the business image, all franchisees, the system, and the public. If such bargaining away of key controls were common, a franchisor could erode by bits and pieces the standardization and quality controls necessary to protect the public and the system, so that there would remain no good will and national or chain image worth your investment. Also, what you have today could be bargained away tomorrow. If a franchisor will bargain away the quality and standardization controls in order to get your initial cash, you should look elsewhere for a franchise opportunity.

Summary of Final Precautions

A. Don't be rushed into signing a contract or any other documents relating to a franchise promotion. Be wary of pressure for an immediate contract closing. Don't make any deposits or down payments unless you are absolutely certain you are going ahead with the franchise agreement. Remember, reputable firms don't engage in high-pressure tactics.

B. Find out all you can about the franchise. Resolve all areas of uncertainty before making a decision. Ask the franchisor for names and addresses of franchisees. No reputable franchisor will object. Personally contact these franchisees and discuss their operations and whether or not franchisor has fulfilled obligations.

C. Check with your local Better Business Bureau. Ask for a business responsibility report on the franchisor-promoter. If your local Better Business Bureau has no information on the franchisor, contact the National Better Business Bureau, 230 Park Avenue, New York, N.Y. 10017.

D. Be certain all the terms of the agreement are set forth in a written contract which is not weighted unfairly against you.

E. Consult a lawyer and have him review all aspects of the agreement before you sign the contract.

F. Any complaint you have about deceptive franchising practices should be reported to your local or state consumer protection agency or to the Federal Trade Commission. The regional offices of the FTC are listed in Appendix F.[4]

Evaluating a Franchise
The Franchisor

1. For how many years has the firm offering you a franchise been in operation?

2. Has it a reputation for honesty and fair dealing among those who currently hold a franchise?

3. Will the firm assist you with:

a. A management training program?

b. An employee training program?

c. A public relations program?

d. Capital?

e. Credit?

f. Merchandising ideas?

g. Advertising program?

h. Computer services?

4. Will the firm assist you in finding a good location for your new business?

5. Is the franchising firm adequately financed so that it can carry out its stated plan of financial assistance and expansion?

6. Has the franchisor shown you any certified figures indicating exact net profits of one or more going firms which you have personally checked?

7. Is the franchisor a one-man company or a corporation with an experienced management trained in depth (so that there would always be an experienced man at its head)?

8. Exactly what can the franchisor do for you which you cannot do for yourself?

9. Has the franchisor investigated you carefully enough to assure itself that you can successfully operate one of its franchises at a profit both to it and to you?

Checklists for Self-Evaluation

The Franchise

10. Did your lawyer approve the franchise contract after he studied it paragraph by paragraph?

11. Does the franchise call upon you to take any steps which are, according to your lawyer, unwise or illegal in your state, county, or city?

12. Does the franchise give you an exclusive territory for the length of the franchise or can the franchisor sell a second or third franchise in your territory?

13. Is the franchisor connected in any way with any other franchise company handling similar merchandise or service?

14. If the answer to the last question is "yes," what is your protection against this second franchisor organization?

15. Under what circumstances can you terminate the franchise contract and at what cost to you, if you decide for any reason at all that you wish to cancel it?

16. If you sell your franchise, will you be compensated for your goodwill or will the goodwill you have built into the business be lost by you?

YOU—the Franchisee

17. How much equity capital will you have to have to purchase the franchise and operate it until your income equals expenses? Where are you going to get it?

18. Are you prepared to give up some independence of action to secure the advantages offered by the franchise?

19. Do *you* really believe you have the innate ability, training, and experience to work smoothly and profitably with the franchisor, your employees, and your customers?

20. Are you ready to spend much or all of the remainder of your business life with this franchisor, offering his product or service to your public?

Your Market

21. Have you made any study to determine whether the product or service which you propose to sell under franchise has a market in your territory at the prices you will have to charge?

22. Will the population in the territory given you increase, remain static, or decrease over the next five years?

23. Will the product or service you are considering be in greater demand, about the same, or less in demand five years from now?

24. What competition exists in your territory already for the product or service you contemplate selling?

a. Nonfranchise firms?

b. Franchise firms?[5]

Checklist for Going Into Business

Summary People sometimes go into business for themselves without being fully aware of what is involved. Sometimes they're lucky and succeed. More often, they fail because they do not consider one or more of the ingredients needed for business success.

This checklist is designed to help you decide whether you are qualified or have considered the various phases of going into business for yourself. Careful thought now may help you prevent mistakes and avoid losing your savings and time later. Use this list as a starter. Consider each question as it applies to your situation. Check off each question only after you've made an effort to answer it honestly. Before you omit a question, satisfy yourself that it does not apply to your particular situation.

Questions to Consider

Are You the Type?

	Yes	No
1. Have you rated your personal traits, such as leadership, organizing ability, perseverance, and physical energy?	____	____
2. Have you had some friends rate you on these traits?	____	____
3. Have you considered getting an associate whose strong points will compensate for your weak traits?	____	____

What Are Your Chances for Success?

	Yes	No
4. Have you had any actual business experience?	____	____
5. Do you have special technical skills, such as those needed by a plumber, electrician, mechanic, or radio repairman?	____	____
6. Have you obtained some basic management experience working for someone else?	____	____
7. Have you analyzed the recent trend of business conditions (good or bad)?	____	____
8. Have you analyzed business conditions in the city and neighborhood where you want to locate?	____	____
9. Have you analyzed conditions in the line of business you are planning?	____	____
10. Have you determined what size business you plan to establish (dollar sales per year)?	____	____
11. Have you built up a detailed set of figures on how much capital you will need to launch the business?	____	____

What Are Your Chances for Success?	Yes	No
12. Have you figured how much time you will need until the business income equals the expenses?	____	____
13. Have you planned what net profit you believe you should make?	____	____
14. Will the net profit divided by the investment result in a rate of return which compares favorably with the rate you can obtain from other investment opportunities?	____	____

How Much Capital Will You Need?	Yes	No
15. Have you worked out what income from sales or services you can reasonably expect in the first six months? The first year? The second year?	____	____
16. Do you know what net profit you can expect on these volumes?	____	____
17. Have you made a conservative forecast of expenses, including a regular salary for yourself?	____	____
18. Have you compared this income with what you would make working for someone else?	____	____
19. Are you willing to risk uncertain or irregular income for the next year? Two years?	____	____
20. Have you counted up how much actual money you have to invest in your business?	____	____
21. Do you have other assets which you could sell or on which you could borrow?	____	____
22. Have you some other source from which you could borrow money?	____	____
23. Have you talked to a banker?	____	____
24. Is he favorably impressed with your plan?	____	____
25. Do you have a financial reserve for unexpected needs?	____	____
26. Does your total capital, from all sources, cover your best estimates of the capital you will need?	____	____

Should You Share Ownership with Others?	Yes	No
27. Do you lack technical or management skills which can be most satisfactorily supplied by one or more partners?	____	____

28. Do you need the financial assistance of one or more partners? _____ _____

29. Have you checked the features of each form or organization (individual proprietorship, partnership, corporation) to see which will best fit your situation? _____ _____

Where Should You Locate?　　　　　　　　Yes　　No

30. Do you know how much space you will need? _____ _____

31. Do you know what type of building you will need? _____ _____

32. Do you know of any special features you require in lighting, heating, ventilating, air conditioning, or parking facilities? _____ _____

33. Have you listed the tools and equipment you need room for? _____ _____

34. If the proposed location does not meet nearly all your requirements, is there a sound reason why you should not wait and continue seeking a more ideal location? _____ _____

35. Have you checked the U.S. Census Bureau population figures? _____ _____

Should You Buy a Going Business?　　　　Yes　　No

36. Have you considered the advantages and disadvantages of buying a going business? _____ _____

37. Have you compared what it would take to equip and stock a new business with the price asked for the business you are considering? _____ _____

38. Have you learned why the present owner wants to sell? _____ _____

39. Have you checked the owner's claims about the business with reports from an independent accountant's analysis of the figures? _____ _____

40. Have you checked with the company's suppliers to obtain their ideas of the value of the business? _____ _____

41. Do the suppliers think well of the proposition? _____ _____

42. Is the stock of merchandise a questionable buy? (Would a large proportion of it have to be disposed of at a loss? Is any of it out of date, unsaleable, or not usable?) _____ _____

Should You Buy a Going Business? Yes No

43. Are the physical facilities old or in poor condition and, hence, overvalued? _____ _____

44. Are you sure the accounts receivable are worth the asking price? _____ _____

45. Is the present company's good will fairly valued? _____ _____

46. Are you prepared to assume the liabilities, and are the creditors agreeable? _____ _____

47. Has your lawyer checked to see if the title is good and if there is any lien against the assets? _____ _____

48. Are there any back taxes to pay? _____ _____

49. Have the sales been temporarily increased by conditions which are not likely to continue? _____ _____

Are You Qualified to Supervise Buying and Selling? Yes No

50. Have you estimated your total stock requirements? _____ _____

51. Do you know in what quantities users buy your product or service? _____ _____

52. Do you know how often users buy your product or service? _____ _____

53. Have you made a sales analysis to determine major lines to be carried? _____ _____

54. Have you decided what characteristics you will require in your goods? _____ _____

55. Have you set up a model stock assortment to follow in your buying? _____ _____

56. Have you investigated whether it will be cheaper to buy large quantities infrequently or small quantities frequently? _____ _____

57. Have you weighed price differentials for large orders against capital and space tied up? _____ _____

58. Have you decided what merchandise to buy direct from manufacturers? _____ _____

59. Will you make your account more valuable to your suppliers by concentrating your buying with a few of them? _____ _____

60. Have you worked out control plans to ensure stocking the right quantities? _____ _____

How Will You Price Your Products and Services?   Yes   No

61. Have you determined what prices you will have to charge to cover your costs and obtain profits? _____ _____

62. Do these prices compare favorably with prices of competitors? _____ _____

What Selling Methods Will You Use?   Yes   No

63. Have you studied the sales promotion methods used by competitors? _____ _____

64. Have you outlined your own sales promotion policy? _____ _____

65. Have you studied why customers buy your product (service, price, quality, distinctive styling, other)? _____ _____

66. Will you do outside selling? _____ _____

67. Will you advertise in the newspapers? _____ _____

68. Will you do direct-mail advertising? _____ _____

69. Will you use posters and handbills? _____ _____

70. Will you use radio and television advertising? _____ _____

How Will You Manage Personnel?   Yes   No

71. Will you be able to hire satisfactory employees, locally, to supply skills you lack? _____ _____

72. Do you know what skills are necessary? _____ _____

73. Have you checked the prevailing wage scales? _____ _____

74. Have you a clearcut idea of what you plan to pay? _____ _____

75. Have you considered hiring someone now employed by a competitor? _____ _____

76. Have you checked on the pros and cons of doing so? _____ _____

77. Have you planned your training procedures? _____ _____

Checklists for Self-Evaluation

What Records Will You Keep?	Yes	No
78. Have you a suitable bookkeeping system ready to operate?	____	____
79. Have you planned a merchandise control system?	____	____
80. Have you obtained standard operating ratios for your type of business to use as guides?	____	____
81. Have you provided for additional records as necessary?	____	____
82. Have you a system to use in keeping a check on costs?	____	____
83. Do you need any special forms?	____	____
84. Have you made adequate provision for having your record keeping done?	____	____

What Laws Will Affect You?	Yes	No
85. Have you investigated what licenses, if any, are necessary to do business?	____	____
86. Have you checked the health regulations?	____	____
87. Are your operations subject to interstate commerce regulations?	____	____
88. Have you seen your lawyer for advice on how to meet your legal responsibilities?	____	____

What Other Problems Will You Face?	Yes	No
89. Have you worked out a system for handling your tax requirements?	____	____
90. Have you arranged for adequate insurance coverage?	____	____
91. Have you worked out a way of building a management team?	____	____
92. Does your family (if any) agree that your proposed venture is sound?	____	____
93. Do you have enough capital to carry accounts receivable?	____	____
94. Will you sell for credit?	____	____
95. Have you worked out a definite returned-goods policy?	____	____

96. Have you considered other management policies which must be established?   _____ _____

97. Have you planned how you will organize and assign the work?   _____ _____

98. Have you made a work plan for yourself?   _____ _____

Will You Keep Up to Date?   Yes   No

99. Have you a plan for keeping up with new developments in your line of business?   _____ _____

100. Have you a small group of qualified advisers from whom you can get help in solving new problems?   _____ _____

Appendices

Appendix A

Definitions

1. "Advertisement" includes any written or printed communication, or any communication by means of recorded telephone messages or spoken on radio, television, or similar communications media, published in connection with an offer or sale of a franchise.

2. "Department" means the department of law.

3. "Franchise" means a contract or agreement, either expressed or implied, whether oral or written, between two or more persons by which:

a. A franchisee is granted the right to engage in the business of offering, selling, or distributing goods or services under a marketing plan or system prescribed in substantial part by a franchisor, and the franchisee is required to pay, directly or indirectly, a franchise fee, or

b. A franchisee is granted the right to engage in the business of offering, selling, or distributing goods or services substantially associated with the franchisor's trademark, service mark, trade name, logotype, advertising, or other commercial symbol designating the franchisor or its affiliate, and the franchisee is required to pay, directly or indirectly, a franchisee fee.

A franchise under this article shall not include any agreement, contract, or franchise subject to the provisions of article eleven-B of this chapter or section one hundred ninety-nine of this chapter, or any agreement or contract for the sale of gas.

4. A "franchisee" is a person to whom a franchise is granted.

5. A "franchisor" is a person who grants a franchise.

6. "Area franchise" means a contract for agreement between a franchisor and a subfranchisor whereby the subfranchisor is granted the right, for consideration given in whole or in part for such right, to sell or negotiate the sale of franchises in the name or on behalf of the franchisor; unless specifically stated otherwise, "franchise" includes "area franchise."

7. "Franchise fee" means any fee or charge that a franchisee or subfranchisor is required to pay or agrees to pay directly or indirectly for the right to enter into a business under a franchise agreement or otherwise sell, resell or distribute goods, services, or franchises under such an agreement, including, but not limited to, any such payment for goods or services. The following are not the payment of a franchise fee:

a. The purchase or agreement to purchase goods at a bona fide wholesale price;

b. The payment of a reasonable service charge to the issuer of a credit card by an establishment accepting or honoring such credit card;

c. Amounts paid to a trading stamp company by a person issuing trading stamps in connection with the retail sale of merchandise or services;

d. The purchase or lease, at fair market value, of real property or agreement to so purchase or lease real property necessary to enter into the business or to continue the business under the franchise agreement;

e. The payment of a fee which on an annual basis does not exceed five hundred dollars where the payor receives sales materials of an equivalent or greater value than his payment;

f. The purchase of sales demonstration equipment and materials furnished at cost for use in making sales and not for resale;

g. A lease, license or other agreement by a retailer permitting the lessee, licensee or beneficiary to offer, sell or distribute goods or services on or about the premises occupied by said retailer.

8. "Franchise sales agent" means a person who directly or indirectly engages in the offer or sale of any franchise on behalf of another. Franchisors, subfranchisors, and their employees are not to be considered franchise sales agents.

9. "Franchise salesman" means each and every person employed by a franchisor or franchise sales agent for the purpose of representing such franchisor or franchise sales agent in the offer or sale of any franchise.

10. "Fraud," "fraudulent practice," and "deceit" are not limited to common law fraud or deceit, and include:

a. Any deception, concealment, suppression, device, scheme or artifice employed by a franchisor, franchise sales agent, subfranchisor or franchise salesman to obtain any money, promissory note, commitment or property by any false or visionary pretense, representation or promise;

b. Any material misrepresentation in any registered prospectus filed under this article; or

c. The omission of any material fact in any registered prospectus filed under this article.

11. "Offer" or "offer to sell" includes any attempt to offer to dispose of, or solicitation of an offer to buy, a franchise or interest in a franchise for value. The terms "offer" and "offer to sell" do not include the renewal or extension of an existing franchise where there is no interruption in the operation of the franchised business by the franchisee.

12. a. An offer or sale of a franchise is made in this state when an offer to sell is made in this state, or an offer to buy is accepted in this state, or, if the franchisee is domiciled in this state, the franchised business is or will be operated in this state.

b. An offer to sell is made in this state when the offer either originated from this state or is directed by the offeror to this state and received at the place to which it is directed. An offer to sell is accepted in this state when acceptance is communicated to the offeror from this state.

c. An offer to sell is not made in this state merely because a publisher circulates or there is circulated on his behalf in this state a bona fide newspaper or other publication of general, regular and paid circulation which has had more than two-thirds of its circulation outside this state during the past twelve months, or a radio or television program originating outside this state is received in this state.

13. "Person" means an individual, corporation, partnership, joint venture, association, company, trust, unincorporated organization or other entity and shall include any other person that has a substanial interest in or effectively controls such person, as well as the individual officers, directors, general partners, trustees or other individuals in control of the activities of each such person.

14. "Publish" means publicly to issue or circulate by newspaper, mail, radio or television, or otherwise to disseminate to the public.

15. "Sale" or "sell" includes every contract or agreement of sale, contract to sell, or disposition of, a franchise or interest in a franchise for value.

16. "State" means any state, territory, or possession of the United States, the District of Columbia and Puerto Rico.

17. "Subfranchisor" means a franchisee who has the right to sell or subdivide his franchise to another or others, known as "subfranchisees," while having and retaining all or part of the franchisor's interest or rights under franchise agreements with such subfranchisee. Under this article and in this situation, the subfranchisee shall be considered the franchisee, and both the principal franchisor and the subfranchisor shall be considered the franchisor.

Source: Business Franchise Guide
©1980, Commercial Clearing House, Inc.

Franchise Agreement

THIS AGREEMENT is made and entered into this _____ day of _____,
19_____, by and between QUICKPRINT, INC., an Ohio corporation with offices
at Holland, Ohio (hereinafter referred to as "Franchisor") and _____

_____

(hereinafter referred to as "Franchisee"), whose address is or shall be _____

_____ .

PREAMBLE

WHEREAS, Franchisor, under its trade secrets, trade names and its trade service marks (hereinafter referred to as "Trademarks") has developed and promoted the name "Big Red Q Quickprint Center," identified with the instant printing and copy business; and

WHEREAS, Franchisor has developed, operates and licenses a system of conducting and operating an instant printing and copying business under the name "Big Red Q Quickprint Center (hereinafter sometimes referred to as the "System"); and

WHEREAS, Franchisor licenses and trains others to use the System and operate Big Red Q Quickprint Centers under its Trademarks; and

WHEREAS, the System, through Franchisor's efforts has acquired substantial goodwill and business value; and

WHEREAS, Franchisee desires to be licensed by Franchisor to use the System and to operate a Big Red Q Quickprint Center as hereinafter provided;

NOW THEREFORE, Franchisor and Franchisee agree as follows:

1. Definitions:

1.1 Trademarks: Shall for all purposes of this Agreement be and shall include all service marks, symbols, logos, trademarks, trade names and trade secrets and goodwill pertaining thereto owned and/or under application by Franchisor now and in the future, and used or associated with the system.

1.2 Location: For all purposes of this Agreement location shall mean that location determined after the execution of this Agreement which is mutually acceptable to Franchisor and Franchisee and to which Franchisor gives its consent in writing, at which the business of the Big Red Q Center is to be carried out.

1.3 Franchisee: Shall for all purposes of this Agreement be and shall include all shareholders, stockholders, officers, owners, agents, consultants, partners, joint venturers and employees of the Franchisee, in the event Franchisee shall be a corporation, at the onset of this Agreement, or at any time during the term hereof.

2. Franchisor Agrees, subject to the terms and conditions of this Agreement:

2.1 Location: To secure Franchisee a location subject to section 1.2 and reasonably assist Franchisee in obtaining a real estate lease for said location. Franchisor agrees not to open or license any other Big Red Q Quickprint Center within the area described or outlined on Exhibit "A," which is attached hereto and made a part hereof, without Franchisee's written consent. If Franchisee should find it necessary or desireable to move from the specified location to other premises serving the same geographical area, Franchisee shall submit a written request to Franchisor which shall consent to said relocation provided said new premises are of acceptable quality and said relocation does not violate a similar agreement between Franchisor and any other Franchisee, or consent is secured from such affected Franchisee.

2.2 Training and Instruction: To provide Franchisee and/or its designated manager at a date or dates to be designated by Franchisor with training and instructions in the operation of a Big Red Q Quickprint Center. Such initial training shall be at Franchisor's training facilities for a period of two weeks and shall be without charge to Franchisee. Franchisor shall pay for Franchisee's travel and lodging expenses, but shall not be responsible for entertainment expenses and board incurred by Franchisee during the training period or should distance require Franchisee to travel by airline such expense shall be limited to round-trip airfare (coach or tourist classification). After said initial training period, Franchisor shall provide an additional two weeks training and instruction to Franchisee on the premises at Franchisee's center, which shall be without charge to Franchisee.

2.3 Continuing Assistance: Franchisor shall give continuing advice, guidance and assistance as it may deem reasonably necessary to Franchisee. Franchisor shall furnish training courses, workshops, and seminars for additional personnel of Franchisee at prices uniformly offered to its Franchisees, and consultation and advice to Franchisee provided that Franchisor shall be paid travel expenses for personnel who visit Franchisee's premises at Franchisee's request. As additional techniques in marketing and/or managing are developed by Franchisor, Franchisor shall make such techniques available to Franchisee through additional training courses, mail distributions or visitation to Franchisee's premises.

2.4 Manual: Franchisor shall provide to Franchisee Franchisor's Management and Operations Manual. In no event shall Franchisee be obligated to comply with or maintain any prices which may be suggested in the manual or any other literature distributed by Franchisor and does not by the execution of this Agreement or the acceptance of the license granted hereby agree to so obligate itself. Except as provided in Paragraphs 3.4 and 4.3 hereof, the Management and Operations Manual is provided to Franchisee with the understanding that it is intended for purposes of guidance only, and that the failure of the Franchisee to follow any suggestions outlined therein shall not, in itself, be grounds for termination of this Agreement. The Franchisee is under no obligation to accept any suggested prices of the Franchisor, and may sell at any price the Franchisee chooses to. If the Franchisee chooses to sell at prices other than those suggested, Franchisee will not suffer in any way in Franchisee's business relations with Franchisor or any other person.

2.5 Trademarks: Franchisor shall make available to Franchisee, Franchisor's names and marks, including trade name and/or trademarks Big Red Q Quickprint Center, and other trademarks to be used in a descriptive manner in the operation of Franchisee's Center. Franchisee shall not form a corporation or other business entity which uses in its name any reference to any trade names, trademarks, or names or marks of Franchisor. The right granted to Franchisee to use the trademarks applies only to their use in connection with the operation of the Big Red Q Quickprint Center, and no other business operation whatsoever. Franchisee agrees during the term of the license agreement and after termination or exportation thereof, not to dispute or contest the validity or enforceability of the trademarks, nor to counsel or procure or assist anyone else to do the same. Franchisee agrees to notify Franchisor of litigation involving said trademarks. Franchisee shall use the trademarks without any accompanying words or symbols and only as prescribed by Franchisor. Franchisee shall affix a notice at a prominent place at the center indicating that the trademarks are owned by Quickprint, Inc. and that the franchised operator of the premises is a licensee of such trademarks.

2.6 Secrecy: Franchisor shall disclose to Franchisee all aspects of the System necessary for the operation of Franchisee's Center and shall keep Franchisee advised of new developments and improvements in the System. Franchisee agrees to keep confidential at all times said System, including, without limitation, the manual of business practices and policies or operations manual made available by Franchisor and not to copy, publish or otherwise duplicate same or permit others to do so and to disclose same only in the ordinary course of business and only to the extent necessary therefore to employees of Franchisee, it being understood that Franchisor shall remain the owner of the Trademarks and System, including, without limitation, said manual and all materials contained therein. Franchisee agrees that failure to adhere to the provisions of this subsection will constitute a material default of this Agreement. Franchisee further acknowledges the impossibility of accurately determining the tangible and intangible damages which Franchisor will suffer from any breach of the provisions against such breach and to pay court costs and reasonable legal fees unless Franchisee should prevail in the suit or proceeding.

2.7 Decor: Franchisor shall provide Franchisee with design and decor for Franchisee's Center, and provide to Franchisee a layout for equipment to be installed at Franchisee's Center. Franchisor shall provide specifications for equipment and furniture to be used in the operation of Franchisee's center all of which are set forth in Exhibit "B" attached hereto and made a part hereof.

2.8 Equipment: Franchisor shall render reasonable assistance to Franchisee in obtaining the equipment recommended by Franchisor for the proper performance of Franchisee's Center as listed in Exhibit "B"; provided, however, any financing assistance as may be required shall be arranged by separate agreement between Franchisor and Franchisee. Title to all signs which bear any trademark of Franchisor shall remain in Franchisor.

2.9 Initial Operating Supplies: Franchisor shall deliver to Franchisee an initial supply of the paper and other items listed on Exhibit "C" attached hereto.

2.10 Other Supplies and Equipment: Franchisor shall exert its best efforts to make available at all times for purchase by Franchisee, bags, imprinted tapes, packaging and wrapping materials and other supplies required by Franchisee in the operation of its Center. To the extent feasible, Franchisor will issue minimum specifications for quality and uniformity for all supplies as needed by Franchisee. Franchisee may purchase such supplies as needed from Franchisor or any other source as long as supplies obtained from sources other than Franchisor meet Franchisor's minimum specifications for imprints and quality. Franchisor reserves the right to require samples of such proposed alternately sourced supplies be submitted to it prior to use, and to have the opportunity to have the supplies tested by an independent testing laboratory. Consent to an alternate source of supply, or type of equipment or material will not be unreasonably withheld.

3. Franchisee Agrees:

3.1 Franchise Fee: Consideration for the granting of the Franchisee herein shall be _____ which shall constitute the franchise fee. Upon execution of this Agreement Franchisee shall pay the franchisor the sum of _____. The sole consideration for payment of the franchise fee is the entering into by the Franchisor of the license agreement, and the fee is deemed to be fully earned, and non-refundable upon execution of the agreement.

3.2 Service Fee: Franchisee shall pay to Franchisor on or before the 7th business day of each month during the term of this Agreement a service fee in an amount equal to five percent (5%) of the gross sales of Franchisee's Big Red Q Quickprint Center for the month preceding. Gross sales in each month shall include all fees, whether paid in cash, or charged, made in connection with sales transacted and services rendered to customers of Franchisee's Center. Gross sales shall not include sales taxes levied or other similar government charges.

Franchisee agrees that in the event the service fee is received by Franchisor after the 7th business day of each month that Franchisor shall have the option to charge for each day that the payment is overdue a late charge of five dollars ($5.00) per day. Any late charge which is assessed by Franchisor shall be invoiced to the Franchisee for payment with the next monthly service fee. In the event any late charge is not paid with the next monthly service fee payment, then Franchisor may, at its option, deem that monthly service fee payment to be late and late payment charges may continue to be assessed until all monthly service fee payments and any late charges have been brought to a current basis.

Franchisee agrees to punctually pay all amounts due Franchisor and further, all amounts owed to others by Franchisee the payment of which Franchisor has guaranteed.

In the event Franchisee is incorporated, or transfers this license to a corporation, the Franchisee must provide that its officers and/or shareholders will guarantee full, prompt, and complete performance by Franchisee of all the terms, covenants and conditions of this agreement made by Franchisee with the Franchisor and the payment of all sums that may become due to the Franchisor from the Franchisee. The undersigned individuals hereby agree to do so.

This guaranty is not limited to any particular period of time but shall continue until all of the terms, convenants and conditions of this agreement have been fully and completely performed by the Franchisee or otherwise discharged by the Franchisor, and the Guarantor(s) shall not be released of any obligation or liability hereunder so long as there is any claim of the Franchisor against the Franchisee arising out of this agreement that has not been settled or discharged in full.

In the event that the Franchisee shall fail to perform any of the terms, covenants and conditions of this agreement as to which such default has occurred in the same manner and as fully as the Franchisee might do.

Each Guarantor hereby waives notice of acceptance of this Agreement.

In the event that the Franchisee shall fail to perform any of the terms, covenants and conditions of this agreement, the Franchisor shall at once give notice to the Guarantor of such default and shall afford to the Guarantor the opportunity to perform as hereinbefore provided.

3.3 Advertising: Franchisee shall insert a display advertisement in the local yellow pages wherein its Center is located or, if requested by Franchisor, participate in a multiple insertion if there is more than one Franchisee in the area. Franchisor shall have the right, in the event Franchisee's location makes combination advertising with other franchisees in the same city, newspaper circulation area or radio broadcasting area to be efficient and productive, to require Franchisee's local advertising to be combined with one or more other Franchisees in such area, and to approve the media selection and format. All local advertising, whether individual or combined, shall prominently display the name Big Red Q Quickprint Center, its trademarks and logos. Franchisor shall make available to Franchisee from time to time such advertising copy mats, radio and television tapes and other local display suggestions as it or its other Franchisees may develop, at Franchisor's costs, however, Franchisee shall not be obligated to accept or purchase same. Franchisee agrees to expend during each month of the term hereof, in addition to any amount expended in advertising in local yellow pages, an amount equal to the greater of $150.00 or 3% of Franchisee's gross sales for the immediately preceding month. All local advertising shall display the trademarks only in such form as may be approved by Franchisor, and no such local advertising may be undertaken without the prior written approval of Franchisor, unless those advertising copy mats, radio and television tapes, and other local display suggestions furnished by Franchisor are used.

3.4 Best Efforts: Franchisee shall devote best efforts to the operation of Franchisee's Center at maximum capacity and efficiency, maintaining a high quality of work and services, employing sufficient help to do same, remaining open for business continuously at least five days per week throughout the year, legal holidays excluded, during normal business hours in the locality where Franchisee's Center is located (except when premises at Franchisee's Center are rendered untenantable for a period not to exceed one hundred twenty (120) days by reason of fire and other casualty). Franchisee expressly recognizes Franchisor's interest in maintaining the continued reputation and goodwill of Franchisor and Franchisee agrees at all times to abide by reasonable policies, rules and regulations of Franchisor which are designed to protect Franchisor's trademarks and the reputation and goodwill associated therewith; to maintain the interior and exterior of the premises in a clean, orderly condition; and to keep in good repair and maintain in accordance with specifications of the Franchisor all signs or displays using any of the Franchisor's trademarks. In the event Franchisee shall fail to maintain his business premises, signs or displays in proper conditions Franchisor may restore the premises, signs or displays to their proper condition and charge Franchisee for Franchisor's expenses. Franchisee's Center shall be open to inspection at all reasonable times to enable Franchisor to inspect the Center and confer with Franchisee, without receiving the prior consent of Franchisee. Franchisee agrees not to conduct any other business at its Center or to utilize any other trademarks, service marks, logo type or trade name, either alone or in conjunction with any trademarks of Franchisor, without the prior written consent of Franchisor. Any such written consent shall be effective only so long as the operation of another business or use of other trademarks does not materially interfere with effective operation of Franchisee's Big Red Q Quickprint Center.

3.5 Books and Records: Franchisee shall keep true and accurate books of account, which shall be open at all times to Franchisor's reasonable inspection, and shall be subject to audit by Franchisor, during normal business hours. Said books of account shall incorporate or be consistent with the standard bookkeeping system, furnished by Franchisor. Franchisee shall furnish to Franchisor on or before the 7th business day of each month a report of receipts and expenditures of its operation for the immediately preceding month. In the event that any audit by Franchisor shall reveal that Franchisee's payment of the monthly service fee has been less than five percent (5%) of its gross sales then Franchisor may, at its option, charge Franchisee the reasonable expenses of the audit. Franchisee shall also furnish to Franchisor annually a copy of any federal tax returns required to be filed by Franchisee within fifteen (15) days of the filing of any such return, certified to be a true copy by the person preparing such returns and Franchisee shall furnish Franchisor copies of annual financial statements (balance sheets and statements of profit and loss), pertaining to Franchisee's Big Red Q Quickprint

Center prepared by or for Franchisee, promptly upon their completion. In addition, Franchisee shall furnish Franchisor, at least quarterly, with a statement of its profit and loss, said statement to be prepared and furnished to Franchisor within 30 days of the end of the calendar quarter. Upon Franchisor's reasonable request, but not more frequently than monthly Franchisee shall furnish Franchisor a current statement of Franchisee's accounts payable showing the date each item payable is or was due.

3.6 Opening: Franchisor will provide an initial advertising kit as listed on Exhibit "D." In connection with the opening Franchisor will provide assistance in obtaining and coordinating opening advertising. Franchisor agrees to assist Franchisee in the promotion of the opening of the Center. Franchisee agrees to maintain the minimum stock levels of supplies listed on Exhibit "C" at all times. As a condition to opening Franchisee agrees to have working capital, over and above the investment in equipment set forth in Exhibit "B," and any payment required to be made to Franchisor pursuant to the terms of this Agreement in an amount not less than Ten Thousand Dollars. Franchisee expressly acknowledges that the aforesaid working capital figure is a minimum requirement, and that Franchisee may find it advantageous from time to time to obtain additional working capital for the operation of Franchisee's Center.

3.7 Symbols, Logos and Marks: Franchisee expressly recognizes and agrees that the name Big Red Q Quickprint Center together with all Trademarks and goodwill pertaining thereto are, and shall remain, the sole property of the Franchisor and that they have substantial value. Franchisee acknowledges that it has no right, title or interest in the Trademarks, and that upon termination of the license agreement, or any registered user agreement referred to herein, Franchisee shall not be entitled to use the trademarks, and no monetary amount shall be assigned as attributable to any goodwill associated with Franchisee's use of the trademarks upon expiration or termination of the license agreement.

3.8 Expenses and Taxes: Franchisee agrees that he shall be solely responsible for all the expense of the aforesaid Center and for taxes and for levies of any and all kinds in connection with said Big Red Q Quickprint Center and the income therefrom, and the Franchisor shall not be liable for any such expenses, taxes, or levies, or disbursements otherwise paid and incurred in connection with the establishment and maintenance of the aforesaid Center, and the Franchisee agrees to indemnify and save Francisor harmless from any and all claims, lawsuits, demands, actions and causes of action that may arise or be asserted against Franchisor by reason of the establishment and maintenance of the aforesaid Center and to pay all counsel fees and expenses in defending same. It is understood and agreed that in granting this license, the Franchisor does not authorize or empower Franchisee to use the name Big Red Q Quickprint Center or the Trademarks in any other capacity than is provided herein or to sign the name Big Red Q Quickprint Center or Quickprint to any contracts, documents, bills, checks, drafts, notes, mortgages, bonds, leases, bills of sale, or any other instruments of writing, or to hold himself out as a partner or a general or special agent of Franchisor, and Franchisor agrees that all contracts that he may enter into in the establishment and maintenance of said Center shall be in his own name.

3.9 Indemnifications: Franchisee agrees to indemnify and save Franchisor harmless from and against any liability of whatsoever kind and nature arising from or out of any damages or injury to any person, including, but not limited to customers, employees of Franchisee, employees of Franchisor and members of the public, suffered and incurred in or about Franchisee's store or in connection with any or all of Franchisee's activities hereunder. Franchisee agrees to keep in full force and effect Public Liability Insurance with limits of not less than $100,000.00 for one death or injury to one person, and $300,000.00 for death or injury to more than one person in any accident. Additionally, Franchisee shall maintain property damage liability insurance in the amount of $25,000.00 and contents insurance in the amount of $25,000.00. Franchisee agrees to name the Franchisor as an additional insured in the insurance policies required to be obtained.

3.10 Other Obligations: Franchisee agrees to maintain adequate Workmen's Compensation and Employer's Liability Insurance, and to pay any and all taxes, and all other payments required to be made by the laws of the United States or of the state in which the Franchisee's Center is located, including, but not limited to, payments for unemployment insurance, social security, as the case may be, and health insurance in respect of any employees.

3.11 Noncompetition during Term: Franchisee will not have any interest, financial or otherwise either directly, as owner, consultant, joint venture, partner, storeholder or employee in any other business of a similar nature to Franchisor's without written permission of Franchisor during the term of this Agreement or any renewal thereof. Franchisee further acknowledges the impossibility of accurately determining the tangible and intangible damages which Franchisor will suffer from any breach of the provisions of this subsection and accordingly agrees to entry of temporary and permanent injunction against such breach.

3.12 Restrictions on Franchisee:

(a) Franchisee shall refrain from any act or acts which may prejudice the validity of the System or Trademarks or Ownership of Franchisor to the System and Trademarks, either during the term of the license agreement or after expiration or termination thereof for any reason whatsoever.

(b) Franchisee will at all times recognize the validity of the Trademarks and the ownership thereof of Franchisor and the exclusive right and jurisdiction of Franchisor to control the use of the Trademarks and to take all appropriate measures for their protections, and will not at any time put in issue the validity of the Trademarks or ownership thereof and will faithfully observe and execute all the requirements, procedures, and directions of Franchisor touching the use and the safeguarding of the Trademarks.

3.13 Compliance with Local Laws: Franchisee shall utilize the license granted hereunder in strict compliance with all applicable laws, ordinances, regulations, and other requirements of any federal, provincial, municipal, or other government and will obtain all necessary permits, licenses, or other consents for the use of the license granted hereunder.

4. Term, Renewal and Termination:

4.1 Term: Unless terminated by an event described in sections 4.3 or 4.4. this Agreement shall continue in effect for twenty (20) years from the date hereof.

4.2 Renewal: Franchisor agrees to renew, and continue to renew, this Agreement for renewal terms of twenty (20) years each without payment by Franchisee of any additional license fee if in Franchisor's reasonable and objective judgment Franchisee has complied with all of its obligations under this Agreement and owns or is able to extend or renew its lease for the location or to secure an alternate location with the territory as approved by Franchisor without excessive interruptions of operations. Such renewal must be requested by Franchisee by written notice of desire to renew delivered to Franchisee not later than six (6) months prior to the expiration of the term of this Agreement of any renewal term then in effect.

4.3 Termination by Franchisor: This Agreement may be terminated by Franchisor upon the occurrence of any of the following events:

(a) Upon the filing of any proceeding in bankruptcy, voluntary or involuntary, by Franchisee, or upon the appointment of a receiver for Franchisee's business who is not discharged within thirty (30) days after his appointment.

(b) The attempted assignment of this Agreement without the prior written consent of Franchisor.

(c) Material default of performance by Franchisee. As used in this Agreement, material default shall include, but not be limited to, the following:

(1) Franchisee's failure to pay all amounts due under this Agreement, or any other amounts due to Franchisor pursuant to the terms of any other lease, sublease, note, or other agreement between Franchisor and Franchisee for a period of fifteen (15) days after written notice of the default shall have been delivered by Franchisor to Franchisee.

(2) Franchisee's failure to perform any other obligation of this Agreement, which default shall continue for a period of thirty (30) days after delivery of written notice of such default to Franchisee by Franchisor.

(3) Franchisee's default under any lease or sublease agreement covering the premises wherein its Center is located which results in the institution of a lawsuit to terminate the lease or sublease.

(4) Franchisee's default in payment of any amounts which Franchisee owes to any party, the payment of which amount has been guaranteed by Franchisor, and such default in payment continues for fifteen (15) days after delivery of written notice to Franchisee by Franchisor.

(d) Conduct by Franchisee of any other printing or duplicating business outside the terms of this Agreement, without Franchisor's prior written consent.

4.4 Termination by Franchisee: This agreement may be terminated by Franchisee effective thirty (30) days after the delivery of written notice by the

Franchisee to Franchisor upon Franchisee's determination to discontinue the printing business, and compliance with the provisions of 4.6 and 4.7 herein.

4.5 Effect of Termination or Expiration: Upon termination or expiration hereof for any reason, all Franchisee's rights hereunder shall terminate.

4.6 Obligations of Franchisee on Expiration or Termination:

(a) Franchisee shall on the effective date of termination or expiration pay to Franchisor all monies then due Franchisor, without set-off or other reduction, and further, shall pay all amounts owed by Franchisee to any other parties, the payment of which amounts Franchisor has guaranteed, whether or not such amounts have matured under the provisions of Franchisee's agreement with said other party; and

(b) Immediately and permanently discontinue the use of the Trademarks and all aspects of the System and the doing of business under any name or in any manner that might tend to give the general public or persons in the trade the impression that this Agreement or any aspect thereof is still in force or that Franchisee is still associated in any way with Franchisor or that Franchisee has any right to sue or practice the System or Trademarks; and

(c) Immediately transfer to Franchisor or as Franchisor directs each telephone listing, post office box or drawer number of Franchisee, and further, Franchisee agrees to execute such documents as may be necessary to effectuate such transfer to Franchisor or any other party designated by Franchisor. Franchisee authorizes Franchisor to direct the telephone company to transfer the telephone listing in accordance with Franchisor's instructions and Franchisee agrees to hold said telephone company harmless from any and all claims or demands against said telephone company arising out of any direction given it by Franchisor to terminate or transfer Franchisee's telephone service; and

(d) Franchisee shall deliver to Franchisor or as Franchisor directs copies of all mail of Franchisee that relates to the business of Franchisee contemplated hereunder; and

(e) Immediately transfer to Franchisor or as Franchisor directs copies of all business records, including those pertaining to customers and employees of Franchisee; and

(f) Immediately return to Franchisor or at Franchisor's direction dispose of all advertising signs, printed matter and all other materials of whatsoever description bearing Big Red Q Quickprint identification.

4.7 Noncompetition following Termination or Expiration: Upon termination or expiration of this Agreement Franchisee agrees that Franchisee will not engage in any business of a similar nature, directly or indirectly, as owner, consultant, joint venturer, partner, stockholder, or employee, competing with Franchisor or any other Franchisee of Franchisor for a period of six (6) months from and after said day, and within a distance of five (5) miles of a business location of Franchisor or any other Franchisee of Franchisor, and that Franchisee will not at any time following said termination or expiration conduct any business of any type under the name Big Red Q Quickprint Center or any variation of said name. Franchisee acknowledges the impossibility of accurately determining the tangible and intangible damages which Franchisor will suffer by the breach of the provisions of this subsection and accordingly agrees to entry of temporary and permanent injunctions against such breach thereof.

5. Ownership, Assignment and Transfer:

5.1 Transfer by Franchisee: Any transfer by Franchisee of his interest shall be subject to the following:

(a) The Franchisee shall not, without first delivering to Franchisor a written request, and without the Franchisor's prior written consent, which shall not be unreasonably withheld voluntarily or involuntarily, by operation of law or otherwise, sell, assign, transfer, convey to any person or firm or to any corporation (whether the shares or a substantial partnership interest therein is owned by him or others) or encumber his interest in this Agreement, and/or the license granted hereby, or in any location lease, or offer to do so or permit or suffer the same, and any purported assignment shall constitute material default hereunder and shall be null and void. Franchisor may require the submission of certain information regarding the proposed transferee which Franchisor deems reasonably necessary to assist it in its investigation of the proposed transferee.

(b) Anything herein to the contrary notwithstanding:

(1) If Franchisee received from a third person or entity and desires to accept a bona fide, written offer to purchase this business, license and interests

herein, Franchisor shall have the option, exercisable within thirty (30) days after written notice and receipt of a copy of such offer, to purchase such business, license and interest, including any location lease, on the same terms and conditions as offered by said third party. If any such third person or entity is of good character, reputation and financial condition, as determined by the sole judgment of Franchisor, then Franchisee's interest may be assigned to him if Franchisor does not exercise its option (subject to the following provisions of this section).

(2) If Franchisee dies, his personal representative may sell and assign his interest herein (or if Franchisee is or shall then be a corporation and its controlling stockholder dies, his personal representative may sell his shares) only with the prior written consent of the Franchisor but it shall not unreasonably withhold consent to sale or assignment to a qualified person who will conform to the Franchisor's training requirements and assume Franchisee's obligations, if of good character and reputation and economic stability from whom a bona fide offer to purchase has been received, provided, the Franchisor shall have the right and option to acquire the decedent's interest in this Agreement and any location lease at the said offered price, said option to be exercised within thirty (30) days after the Franchisor is notified in writing of said bona fide offer.

(3) If the Franchisee dies and his personal representatives have not received (or do not wish to accept) a bona fide offer to sell, and if under controlling local law or the deceased Franchisee's will, his interest in this Agreement and in the Franchisee's business is distributable to heirs or legatees who are members of his immediate family and who otherwise would qualify as assignees under the terms of the preceding provisions of this section, then such attempted assignment by operation of law or will shall not be deemed in violation hereof or consent thereto unreasonably refused; provided, such heirs or legatees accept the conditions imposed in this section on otherwise permitted assignees.

(c) (1) Consent to an assignment otherwise permitted or permissible as reasonable may be refused unless all obligations of Franchisee are assumed by assignee; all prior ascertained or liquidated debts of Franchisee in connection with the licensed business are paid concurrently with assignment; Franchisee is not in default hereunder; assignee agrees to and avails himself of the training required of new Franchisees as hereinafter set forth; assignee is of good character, reputation and economic stability; and the Franchisee, prior to effectiveness of the assignment, pays to the Franchisor the sum of One Thousand, Five Hundred Dollars ($1,500.00) as a transfer expense charge for the Franchisor's reasonable legal and accounting fees, credit and investigation charges incurred as a consequence of such assignment. The consent of assignment shall be conditioned upon the new Franchisee's attendance for a period of two weeks for initial training at Franchisor's international training center and an additional two week training and instruction period to be conducted at Franchisee's center, both to be conducted and the expense for which shall be on Franchisor's then current terms with respect to assignees of Franchisees.

(d) (2) In the event Franchisee is incorporated, this license shall be considered to have been transferred or assigned if a controlling majority of Franchisee's voting shares are transferred or sold, and the new stockholders and/or officers shall be obligated to avail the Franchisee's management personnel of the training required of new Franchisees, as hereinafter set forth, and to retain in Franchisee the good character, reputation and economic stability that was present at the initiation of this license, and the Franchisee, prior to the effectiveness of assignment, shall pay to the Franchisor the sum of One Thousand, Five Hundred Dollars ($1,500.00) as a transfer expense for the Franchisor's reasonable legal and accounting fees, credit and investigation charges incurred as a consequence of such assignment. The continuance of this license after such transfer or sale of a controlling majority of Franchisee's shares shall be conditioned upon the managerial personnel of Franchisee, after such stock transfer, attending for a period of two weeks the initial training of Franchisor's International Training Center and an additional two weeks training and instruction period to be conducted at Franchisee's Center, both to be conducted and the expense for which shall be on Franchisor's then current terms with respect to assignees of Franchisee, and the Franchisee's new stockholders and/or officers signing a personal guaranty similar to that contained herein. Franchisee agrees to prominently place a suitable notation of this paragraph in the form of a restriction on the stock certificates evidencing ownership of this corporation.

6. General Conditions and Provisions:

6.1 Independent Contractors, Previous Agreements, and Previous Course of Dealing: This Agreement shall not be deemed to create any relationship of agency, employment, partnership or joint venture between the parties hereto. No employee engaged by Franchisee shall under any circumstances be deemed to be an employee of Franchisor, and all employees engaged by Franchisee shall be so notified. Upon execution of this Agreement by the parties all previous agreements, contracts, arrangements or understandings of any kind relative to the license herein granted are canceled and all claims and demands thereon are fully satisfied. This Agreement, the documents incorporated by the reference herein, and any schedules hereto, constitute the entire agreement betwen the parties and all prior negotiations, commitments, conditions, representations, warranties, and undertakings are merged herein. There are no oral or written conditions, representations, warranties, undertakings or agreements made by Franchisor, its agents or affiliates to Franchisee relating to the subject matter of this Agreement. No previous course of dealing or usage of trade not specifically set forth in this agreement shall be admissible to explain, modify or contradict this Agreement.

6.2 Notice: Whenever, under the terms of this Agreement, notice is required, the same shall be deemed delivered if delivered by hand to whom intended, or to any adult person employed by Franchisee at Franchisee's center, or upon deposit in a regular Canadian or United States depository for mail delivery, addressed to Franchisee or Franchisor at the addresses set forth above, or at such other addresses as either party may from time to time formally advise the other.

6.3 Terminology: All terms and words used in this Agreement, regardless of the number and gender in which they are used, shall be deemed and construed to include any other number, singular or plural, and any other gender, masculine, feminine, or neuter, as the context or sense of this Agreement or any section, paragraph or clause herein may require, as if such words had been fully and properly written in the appropriate number and gender.

6.4 Arbitration: Any controversy, dispute or question arising out of, in connection with, or in relation to this Agreement or its interpretation, performance or non-performance of any breach thereof shall be determined by arbitration before an arbitrator selected by and in accordance with the rules of the American Arbitration Association. Unless otherwise mutually agreed by Franchisee and Franchisor, all arbitration hearings will be conducted in Toledo, Ohio. The arbitrator selected by the American Arbitration Association shall have the power and jurisdiction to decide such claim or grievance solely in accordance with the express provisions of this Agreement and shall not have the power or jurisdiction to alter, amend, delete or add to such express provisions by implication or otherwise. In any such arbitration, both Franchisee and Franchisor shall be entitled to specific performance of the obligations of the other hereunder. The decision of the arbitrator made within his power or jurisdiction shall be final and binding and enforceable by judgment in any court of law having jurisdiction. The costs of the arbitrator will be shared equally. Provided, however, as a condition precedent to submission of the matter to arbitration the party seeking arbitration shall:

(A) First submit in writing its claim, grievance or dispute arising under the terms of this Agreement to the other party at the address set forth herein; such writing shall recite all of the facts relating to the claim, grievance or dispute and shall include any additional material which the party seeking arbitration believes would be helpful to the other party in evaluating the claim, grievance or dispute;

(B) If the claim, grievance or dispute is not settled within ten (10) days after submission of the writing, unless such time is extended by mutual agreement between the parties, the matter may be submitted to arbitration. Notwithstanding anything in this section 6.4 to the contrary, nothing herein shall in any way deprive, prohibit or limit the Franchisor of its right to obtain injunction or other equitable relief as previously set forth in this Agreement.

6.5 Severability: The paragraphs of this Agreement are severable, and in the event any paragraph or portion of the Agreement is declared illegal or unenforceable, the remainder of the Agreement shall be effective and binding on the parties.

6.6 Waivers: No waiver of any breach of any of the covenants, agreements or provisions herein contained shall be construed as a waiver of any subsequent breach of the same or any other covenant or provision.

6.7 Cumulative Rights and Remedies: All rights and remedies herein conferred upon or reserved to the parties shall be cumulative and concurrent and shall be in addition to every other right or remedy given to the parties herein or at law or in equity or by statute are not intended to be exclusive of any other right or remedy. The termination or expiration of this Agreement shall not deprive the parties of any of their rights or remedies against the other to enforce at law or in equity any of the rights or remedies of either party hereunder.

6.8 Successors: This Agreement shall inure to the benefit of and be binding upon the heirs, successors, personal representatives and permitted assigns of the parties.

6.9 Applicable Law: This Agreement is entered into and shall be construed in accordance with the laws of the State of Ohio, as of the date of execution of this Agreement.

IN WITNESS WHEREOF, each of the undersigned hereby acknowledges having read this Agreement, understands and consents to be bound by all of its terms, and agrees it shall become effective and has been executed this _____ day of _____, 19_____.

QUICKPRINTS, INC., FRANCHISOR

By: _____
Authorized Officer

FRANCHISEE: _____

By: _____
OFFICER/FRANCHISEE/GUARANTOR

By: _____
OFFICER/FRANCHISEE/GUARANTOR

Average Sales Volume—Stores Over One Year Old—Big Red Q

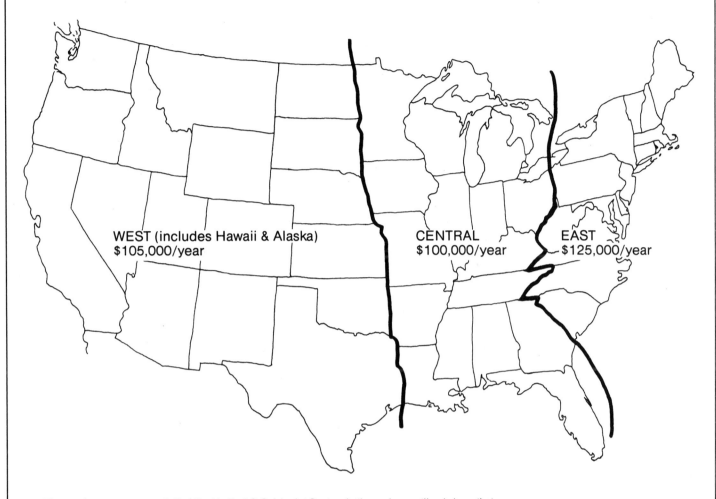

WEST (includes Hawaii & Alaska)
$105,000/year

CENTRAL
$100,000/year

EAST
$125,000/year

These sales are averages of all of the big Red Q Quickprint Centers in the regions outlined above that have been in business more than one year, as of March, 1979, and should not be considered as the actual or potential sales, profits or earnings that will be realized by any other franchise. The Franchisor does not represent that any franchisee can expect to attain these sales, profits or earnings.
Caution: Some outlets have sold this amount. There is no assurance you'll do as well. If you rely upon our figures, you must accept the risk of not doing so well.

Appendix C

State and Federal Laws and Rules Affecting Franchising

	Disclosure				Relationship		
	General	Registration	Gasoline	Bus. Oppor.	General	Vehicles	Gasoline
Alabama						*	
Alaska			*				*
Arizona			*			*	*
Arkansas	*				*	*	*
California	*	*		*	*	*	*
Colorado						*	
Connecticut				*	*		*
Delaware					*		*
Florida	*			*		*	
Georgia				*		*	*
Hawaii	*	*			*	*	*
Idaho						*	
Illinois	*	*			*	*	
Indiana	*	*			*	*	
Iowa						*	*
Kansas						*	*
Kentucky				*	*	*	
Louisiana						*	*
Maine				*		*	*
Maryland	*	*	*	*		*	*
Massachusetts						*	*
Michigan	*	*			*	*	
Minnesota	*	*			*	*	
Mississippi	*				*	*	
Missouri					*	*	
Montana						*	
Nebraska				*	*	*	
Nevada						*	*

	Disclosure				Relationship		
	General	Registration	Gasoline	Bus. Oppor.	General	Vehicles	Gasoline
New Hampshire			*	*		*	
New Jersey					*	*	*
New Mexico						*	*
New York	*	*	*			*	*
North Carolina				*		*	
North Dakota	*	*				*	
Ohio				*		*	
Oklahoma						*	
Oregon	*						
Pennsylvania					*	*	
Rhode Island	*	*				*	*
South Carolina				*		*	
South Dakota	*	*			*	*	
Tennessee			*			*	*
Texas						*	
Utah						*	*
Vermont			*			*	*
Virginia	*	*		*	*	*	*
Washington	*	*			*	*	
West Virginia			*			*	*
Wisconsin	*	*			*	*	
Wyoming						*	
District of Columbia							
Puerto Rico					*		
U.S. Virgin Islands					*		
Alberta	*	*					
Quebec	*	*					
United States						*	*

Source: Franchising Manual Seminar/New York University

FTC Rule and State Laws

Unpreempted Law and Rule Provisions

Charted here are state law and regulation provisions that "arguably" survive the preemptive effect intended of the FTC disclosure rule, either because they are not inconsistent with the rule or because they are more protective of prospective franchisees.

Requirement or Restriction	Calif.	Haw.	Ill.	Ind.	Md.	Mich.	Minn.	N.Y.	N. Dak.	Ore.	R.I.	S. Dak.	Va.	Wash.	Wis.
Registration	x		x	x	x	x	x	x	x		x	x	x	x	x
Oral contracts	x	x	x	x	x	x	x	x	x	x	x	x		x	
Area franchises	x		x			x	x	x	x			x			
Escrow or surety bonds	x		x	x	x	x	x	x	x		x	x	x	x	x
Recordkeeping	x	x	x	x		x	x	x	x	x	x	x		x	x
Franchisee association	x	x	x			x	x	x						x	
Good-faith dealing		x												x	
Purchasing requirements		x		x		x								x	
Discrimination		x	x	x		x	x							x	
Kickbacks		x		x										x	
Exclusive territory		x		x		x	x							x	
Conduct standards		x					x							x	
Good cause termination		x	x	x		x	x						x	x	x
Repurchase/compensation		x	x			x								x	x
Registration of brokers		x	x			x								x	
Identification of offeror	x							x	x			x			
Registration of employed sellers				x											
Statements about state approval			x	x		x			x		x	x		x	x
Covenants not to compete				x			x								
Misuse of franchise fees					x										x
Risk to franchisee				x		x									
Unfair contract terms												x			
Filing of advertisements	x		x	x	x	x	x	x	x		x	x		x	x
Disapproved advertising	x			x		x	x	x				x		x	x
Deceptive advertising			x				x							x	x
Fraud or deception			x		x	x	x								x
Fraudulent registration	x		x			x	x	x	x		x	x		x	x
Fraudulent offers and sales	x	x	x	x		x	x	x	x	x	x	x	x	x	x
Individual liability	x	x	x	x		x		x	x	x	x	x		x	x
Private cause of action	x	x	x	x		x	x	x	x	x	x	x	x	x	x
Release of liability		x		x		x	x							x	
Orders and investigations	x	x	x	x	x	x	x	x	x	x	x	x	x	x	x
Violations of orders						x				x		x			
State suits	x	x	x	x	x	x	x	x	x	x	x	x	x	x	x
Criminal penalties	x	x	x	x		x		x	x		x	x	x	x	x
Lower franchise fee	x	x		x	x		x	x	x		x	x	x	x	x
Disposition of franchise	x		x	x	x	x	x	x	x		x	x		x	x

FTC Rule v. State Laws

Preempted Law and Rule Provisions

Charted here are state law and regulation provisions that "arguably" do not survive preemptive effects intended of the FTC disclosure rule, either because they are inconsistent with the rule or because they are less protective of prospective franchisees.

	Calif.	Haw.	Ill.	Ind.	Md.	Mich.	Minn.	N.Y.	N. Dak.	Ore.	R.I.	S. Dak.	Va.	Wash.	Wis.
Disclosure time	x	x	x	x	x	x	x	x	x	x	x	x	x	x	x
Exemption, exclusion Large franchisor	x		x		x		x		x		x	x		x	x
Large franchisee						x									
Limited offering														x	
Petroleum	x							x							
Motor vehicle (but see FTC options)		x												x	
Vehicle lessors														x	
Farm equip. motor and RV												x			
Insurance														x	
Cable TV															x
Sale to financial firm		x	x		x	x						x		x	
Securities registered in state							x					x			
Loan to franchisee repaid 6 mos.		x		x			x					x		x	
Purchase or lease of needed supplies		x					x					x		x	
Equipment purchase/rent $500 in 1st 6 mos.	x			x				x							
Sales materials					x										
Fee under $100 but $500 paid in 6 mos.															x
New pact on franchisee sale						x									
Wholesale price for non-resale goods	x	x	x	x	x		x	x	x		x	x		x	x
Foreign franchisee		x													

Source: Franchising Manual Seminar New York University

Appendix E

State Officials Responsible for Franchise Registration

The following is a list of state officials having responsibility for administering franchise registration and disclosure laws, together with reference to regulations, if any, issued under such laws:

State	Official	Regulations
California	Commissioner of Corporations	California Administrative Code, Title 10, Chapter 3, Subchapter 2.6
Florida		None
Hawaii	Director of Regulatory Agencies	None
Illinois	Attorney General	Rules and Regulations, Uniform Franchise Registration Application and Special Bulletin No. 1 (Statement of Policy) available from Franchise Division, Office of the Attorney General, 500 South Second Street, Springfield, Ill. 62706
Indiana	Securities Commissioner	None
Maryland	Securities Commissioner Law Department	Proposed Regulations: 4:26 Maryland Register 2005–2021 (Dec. 16, 1977), 5:5 Maryland Register 327–334 (March 10, 1978), affecting Code of Maryland Regulations COMAR 02.02.04
Michigan	Director of Commerce Corporation and Securities Bureau	Michigan Administrative Code 1954, Supplement No. 87, R 445-101-R445-901
Minnesota	Commissioner of Securities Department of Commerce	Minnesota Code of Agency Rules, Minnesota Regulations, Securities Division 1701–1722a
Mississippi	Attorney General	None
New York	Attorney General	N.Y. General Business Article 33, Sections 680–695, added by Laws of 1980 Chapters 730, 731.
North Dakota	Commissioner of Securities	None
Oregon	Corporation Commissioner	Oregon Administrative Rules, Chapter 815, Davison 40, 815-40-000-815-40-070
Rhode Island	Director of Business Regulation	None
South Dakota	Director of the Division of Securities	None
Virginia	State Corporation	Application for Registration, Consent to Service of Process, and Franchisor's Surety Bond available Shockoe Center Building, 11 South 12th Street, Richmond, Va. 23219
Washington	Director of Department of Motor Vehicles, Securities Division	Washington Administrative Code, Chapter 460–80
Wisconsin	Commissioner of Securities	Wisconsin Administrative Code, Section SEC32

Exemption from registration under most state laws requiring preregistration is permitted if the franchisor has a substantial net worth (usually $5,000,000 based on audited financials), has had a number of franchises operating during a five-year period, or continuously conducted the business which is the subject of franchise for a five-year period, and provides disclosure statements to each prospective franchisee.

Federal Trade Commission Assistance The Commission has prepared proposed interpretative guidelines to the Rule in an effort to assist franchisors and franchise brokers in complying with the Rule. These interpretative guidelines are open for public comment through February 20, 1979. Final interpretative guidelines will be issued after a review of comments received, and prior to the effective date of the Rule.

The Commission will furnish a formal advisory opinion, about the relationship of the Rule, to specific fact situations in accordance with its Procedures and Rule of Practice.

The Commission's franchise staff will furnish informal staff opinions, in appropriate circumstances, upon written request.

Regional Offices:

Regional Director
730 Peachtree Street NE, Rm. 720
Atlanta, GA 30308
(404) 526-5836

Regional Director
John Fitzgerald Kennedy Federal
Building
Government Center
Boston, MA 02203
(617) 223-6621

Regional Director
Room 486
Everett M. Dirkson Office Building
219 South Dearborn Street
Chicago, ILL 60604
(312) 353-4423

Regional Director
Federal Office Building, Rm. 1339
1240 East 9th Street
Cleveland, OH 44199
(216) 522-4207

Regional Director
911 Walnut Street
2806 Federal Office Building
Kansas City, MO 64106
(816) 374-5256

Regional Director
11000 Wilshire Boulevard, Rm. 13209
Los Angeles, CA 90024
(213) 824-7575

Regional Director
1000 Masonic Temple Building
333 St. Charles Street
New Orleans, LA 70130
(504) 527-2091

Regional Director
22nd Floor Federal Building
26 Federal Plaza
New York, NY 10007
(212) 264-1200

Notes

1. How to Own Your Own Business with Limited Capital

1. Carl McDaniel, Jr., *Marketing: An Integrated Approach* (New York: Harper & Row, 1979), p. 253.

2. Ibid., p. 254.

3. U.S. Senate, 91st Congress, 2nd Session, Report #91–1344 (Washington, D.C.: U.S. Government Printing Office, 1970), p. 7.

4. J. F. Atkinson, *Franchising: The Odds-On Favorite* (Chicago: International Franchise Association., 1968), p. 3.

5. The Conference Board, *Franchised Distribution*, p. 1.

6. Charles L. Vaughn, *Franchising* (Lexington, Mass.: D.C. Heath, 1979), rev., p. 9.

7. Lee Smith, "Burger King Puts Down Its Dukes," *Fortune* (June 16, 1980), p. 90.

8. Vaughn, op. cit., p. 2.

9. Vaughn, op. cit., p. 5–8.

10. *Susser v Carvel Corp.*, 206 F. Supp. 636 (S.D.N.Y. 1962).

2. Energizing the Economy

1. U.S. Department of Commerce, *Franchising in the Economy, 1978–1980* (Jan. 1980), p. 1.
   All other data in this chapter are drawn from the same source unless otherwise stated.

2. J. K. Atkinson, *Franchising: The Odds-On Favorite* (Chicago: International Franchise Association, 1968), p. 5.

3. Thomas C. Buckhart, vice-president, Ben Franklin Stores, Des Plaines, Ill. Personal interview (Sept. 16, 1980).

4. Command Performance news release for business editors, Sept. 9, 1980.

5. *Entrepreneur* (March 1980), pp. 43–44.

3. The Advantages and Disadvantages of Franchising

1. Charles L. Vaughn, *Franchising*, p. 22, 37.

2. *U.S. News and World Report* (June 11, 1979), p. 7.

3. A. J. Vogel, "Franchising: The New American Dream," *Sales Management*, (May 15, 1964), p. 89.

4. Perry Mendel, "Perry Mendel's Golden Diapers," *Forbes* (June 25, 1979), p. 67.

5. Chase Revel, "Should You Franchise Your Business?" *Entrepreneur* (March 1980), p..119–120.

6. Vaughn, op. cit., p. 73.

7. John M. Ivanevich, Herbert L. Lyon, and David P. Adams, *Business in a Dynamic Environment*, p. 119.

8. J. T. Atkinson, *Franchising: The Odds-On Favorite*, p. 32.

9. Vaughn, op. cit., p. 73.

10. Harold Brown, *Franchising: Trap for the Trusting*, p. 6.

4. The Franchise Agreement

1. U.S. Department of Commerce, *Franchising in the Economy, 1977–1979*, pp. 9–10.

2. J.A.H. Curry, et al., *Partners for Profit* (New York: American Management Association, 1969), p. 32.

3. Harold Brown, *Franchising: Trap for the Trusting*, p. 6.

4. David D. Seltz, *How to Get Started in Your Own Franchised Business*, p. 28.

5. The Conference Board, *Franchised Distribution*, p. 55.

6. Harry Kursh, *The Franchise Boom*, p. 101.

7. Ibid., p. 10.

8. Ibid., p. 105.

9. Lee Smith, "Burger King Puts Down Its Dukes," *Fortune* (June 16, 1980), pp. 91–92.

10. Ibid.

11. Robert M. Dias and Stanley I. Gurnick, *Franchising: An Investor's Complete Handbook*, p. 85.

12. The Conference Board, op. cit., p. 58.

13. Kursh, op. cit., p. 107.

14. Gerrold G. Van Cise, *A Franchise Contract* (Washington, D.C.: International Franchise Association, N.D.) p. 14.

15. Dias and Gurnick, op. cit., p. 86.

5. Finding and Evaluating Franchising Opportunities

1. The Conference Board, *Franchised Distribution*, p. 33.

2. Ibid., p. 33.

3. Ibid., p. 33.

4. Ibid., p. 34.

5. Ibid., p. 34.

6. Ibid., p. 34.

7. Ibid., pp. 34, 36.

8. Ibid., p. 39.

9. David M. Dias and Stanley I. Gurnick, *Franchising: An Investor's Complete Handbook*, p. 31.

10. U.S. Department of Commerce, *Franchising in the Economy, 1978–1980*.

6. Franchise Financing

1. Lee Smith, "Burger King Puts Down Its Dukes," *Fortune* (June 16, 1980), pp. 93–94.

2. Marcella Rosene, "Franchise Entrepreneurs of the 1980's," *Venture* (July 1980), p. 27.

3. David Seltz, "Franchise Financing Ideas," N.Y.U. *How to Franchise NYU Seminar Manual*, 1977–80 update. pp. 232–233.

4. "Where to Find the Money for Your Franchise," *Entrepreneur* (March 1980), p. 73.

5. James H. Marx and Lonnie Murray, Private interview (April 19, 1979).

7. Franchising and the Law

1. U.S. Congress, Report of the Select Committee on Small Business, U.S. Senate, "Impact of Franchising on Small Business." Report No. 91-1344, p. 2.

2. U.S. Department of Commerce, *Franchising in the Economy, 1977–1979,* January 1979, p. 21.

3. Ibid.

4. Ibid.

5. Ibid., p. 22.

6. Ibid., p. 24.

7. N.Y.U. Seminar Manual on Franchising, 1980, p. 530

8. U.S. Department of Commerce, op. cit., p. 29.

9. Stanley B. Bernstein, personal interview, New York (Aug. 22, 1980).

10. Vernon W. Haas, *Franchise Law Summary,* 1977, pp. 3–14.

11. Michael J. Brody, personal interview (May 24, 1979).

10. Checklists for Self-Evaluation

1. C. R. Stigelman, "Franchise Index/Profile," Small Business Management Series, No. 35, p. 2.

2. Jerome L. Fels, *Investigate before Investing,* p. 6. All other data in this chapter are drawn from the same source unless otherwise stated.

3. Federal Trade Commission, *Franchise Business Risks,* Consumer Bulletin #4, unpaginated.

4. Ibid.

5. Dr. Wilford L. White, Director, Small Business Guidance and Development Center, Howard University, Washington, D.C. 20001.

Selected Bibliography

Books

Bell, Daniel. *The Coming of Post-Industrial Society* (New York: Basic Books, 1973).

Brown, Harold. *Franchising: Realties and Remedies* (New York: Law Journal Press, 1973).

_____. *Franchising: Trap for the Trusting* (Boston: Little, Brown, 1969).

Dias, Robert M. and Stanley I. Gurnick. *Franchising: An Investor's Complete Handbook* (New York: Hastings House, 1969).

Glickman, Gladys. *Franchising* (New York: Matthew Bender, 1976), rev.

Gross, Harry and Robert S. Levy. *Franchise Investigation: A Contract Negotiation* (New York: Pilot Industries, 1967).

Ivanevich, John M., Herbert L. Lyon, and David P. Adams. *Business in a Dynamic Environment* (New York: West Publishing, 1979).

Kursh, Harry. *The Franchise Boom* (Englewood Cliffs, N.J.: Prentice Hall, 1968).

Lewis, Mack A. *How to Franchise Your Business* (New York: Pilot Industries, 1974).

Scherer, Donald J. *Financial Security and Independence through a Small Business Franchise* (New York: Pilot Industries, Inc., 1978), rev.

Seltz, David D. *How to Get Started in Your Own Franchised Business* (New York: Farnsworth Publishing, 1967).

_____, and Alfred J. Modica. *Negotiate Your Way to Success* (New York: Farnsworth Publishing, 1980).

Vaughn, Charles L. *Franchising: Its Nature, Scope, Advantages and Development* (Lexington, Mass.: D.C. Heath, 1974).

_____. *Franchising* (Lexington, Mass.: D.C. Heath, 1979), rev.

World Future Society, *The Study of the Future* (Washington, D.C., 1977)

Reports and Pamphlets

Atkinson, J. F. *Franchising: The Odds-On Favorite* (Chicago: International Franchise Association, 1968).

Checklist for Going into Business. Small Business Administration, Small Marketers Aid No. 71 (Washington, D.C.: U.S. Government Printing Office, rev. August 1970).

Directory of Franchising Organization. Rev. annually (New York: Pilot Industries, Inc., 1979).

Fels, Jerome L. *Investigate before Investing: Guidance for Prospective Franchisees*. (Washington, D.C.: International Franchise Association, 1971).

The Franchise Annual (Lewiston, New York: Info Press, Inc. Center Street, 14092, 1979).

Franchise Business Risks. Federal Trade Commission, Consumer Bulletin No. 4 (Washington, D.C.: U.S. Government Printing Office, 1972).

Franchised Distribution (New York: The Conference Board, 1971).

Franchise Opportunities Handbook. U.S. Department of Commerce (Washington, D.C.: U.S. Government Printing Office, 1978).

Franchising and Antitrust: The Antitrust Problems and Solutions of Distribution through Franchised Outlets and/or Company Owned Outlet. Official Transcript: Sixth Annual Legal and Governmental Affairs (1973).

Franchising in the Economy 1977–1979. U.S. Department of Commerce (Washington, D.C.: U.S. Government Printing Office, 1979).

Franchising: Small Business Reporter (San Francisco: Bank of America, 1978).

Impact of Franchising on Small Business, Report of the Select Committee on Small Business, United States Senate. 91st Congress, 2nd Session. Report No. 91-1344 (Washington, D.C.: U.S. Government Printing Office, 1979).

Stigelman, C. R. "Franchise Index/Profile" Small Business Administration (Washington, D.C.: U.S. Government Printing Office, 1973).

Tunick, A. L. *Are You Ready for Franchising?* Small Business Administration, Small Marketers Aid No. 115 (Washington, D.C.: U.S. Government Printing Office, rep. January 1974).

Selected Bibliography

Interviews

Bernstein, Stanley B. Pearlman Weinberg Tauber and Bernstein. New York, N.Y., Aug. 25, 1980.

Broady, Michael J., assistant commissioner of the Department of Corporations, State of California., May 30, 1979.

Buckhart, Thomas C., vice-president, Ben Franklin Stores, Des Plaines, Ill., Sept. 16, 1980.

Marx, James H., chief, and Lonnie Murray, Capital Development Office of Minority Business Enterprise, U.S. Department of Commerce. Washington, D.C., April 9, 1979.

Seltz, David D., Seltz Franchising Developments, Inc. New York, N.Y., Aug. 18. 1980.

Summers, John C., legal technician, Federal Trade Commission. Washington, D.C., April 4, 1979.

Tifford, John M., Attorney, Bureau of Consumer Protection, Federal Trade Commission. Washington, D.C., April 6, 1979.

Index